STAR
WARS
JANGO FETT
SLAVE I SLAVE I SLAVE I SLAVE I

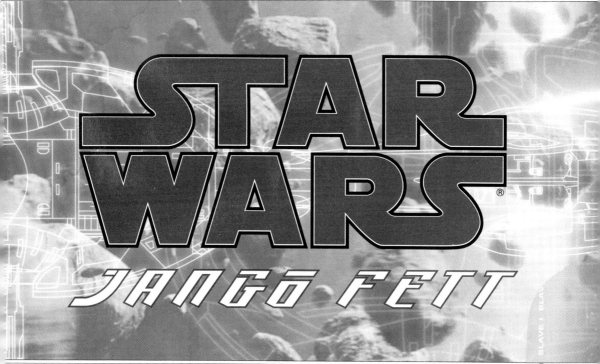

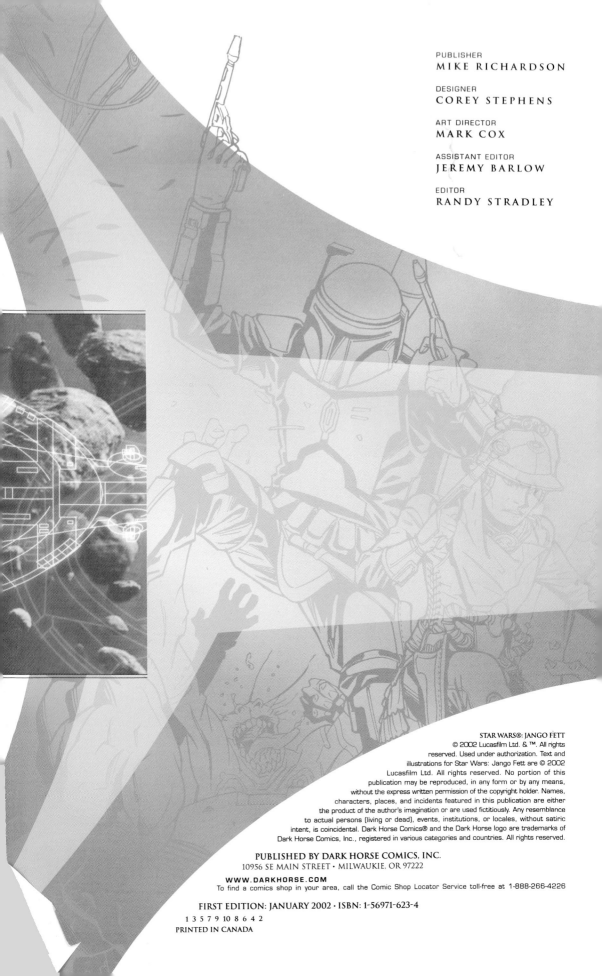

PUBLISHER
MIKE RICHARDSON

DESIGNER
COREY STEPHENS

ART DIRECTOR
MARK COX

ASSISTANT EDITOR
JEREMY BARLOW

EDITOR
RANDY STRADLEY

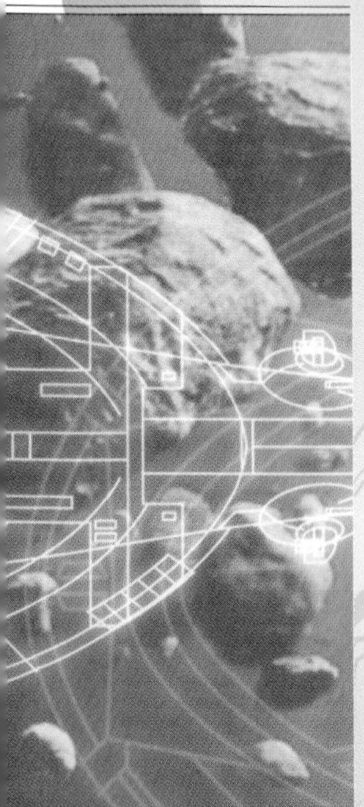

STAR WARS®: JANGO FETT

PUBLISHED BY DARK HORSE COMICS, INC.
10956 SE MAIN STREET • MILWAUKIE, OR 97222

WWW.DARKHORSE.COM
To find a comics shop in your area, call the Comic Shop Locator Service toll-free at 1-888-266-4226

FIRST EDITION: JANUARY 2002 • ISBN: 1-56971-623-4

1 3 5 7 9 10 8 6 4 2
PRINTED IN CANADA

STAR WARS
JANGO FETT

STORY BY	RON MARZ
ART BY	TOM FOWLER
LETTERING BY	DAN JACKSON

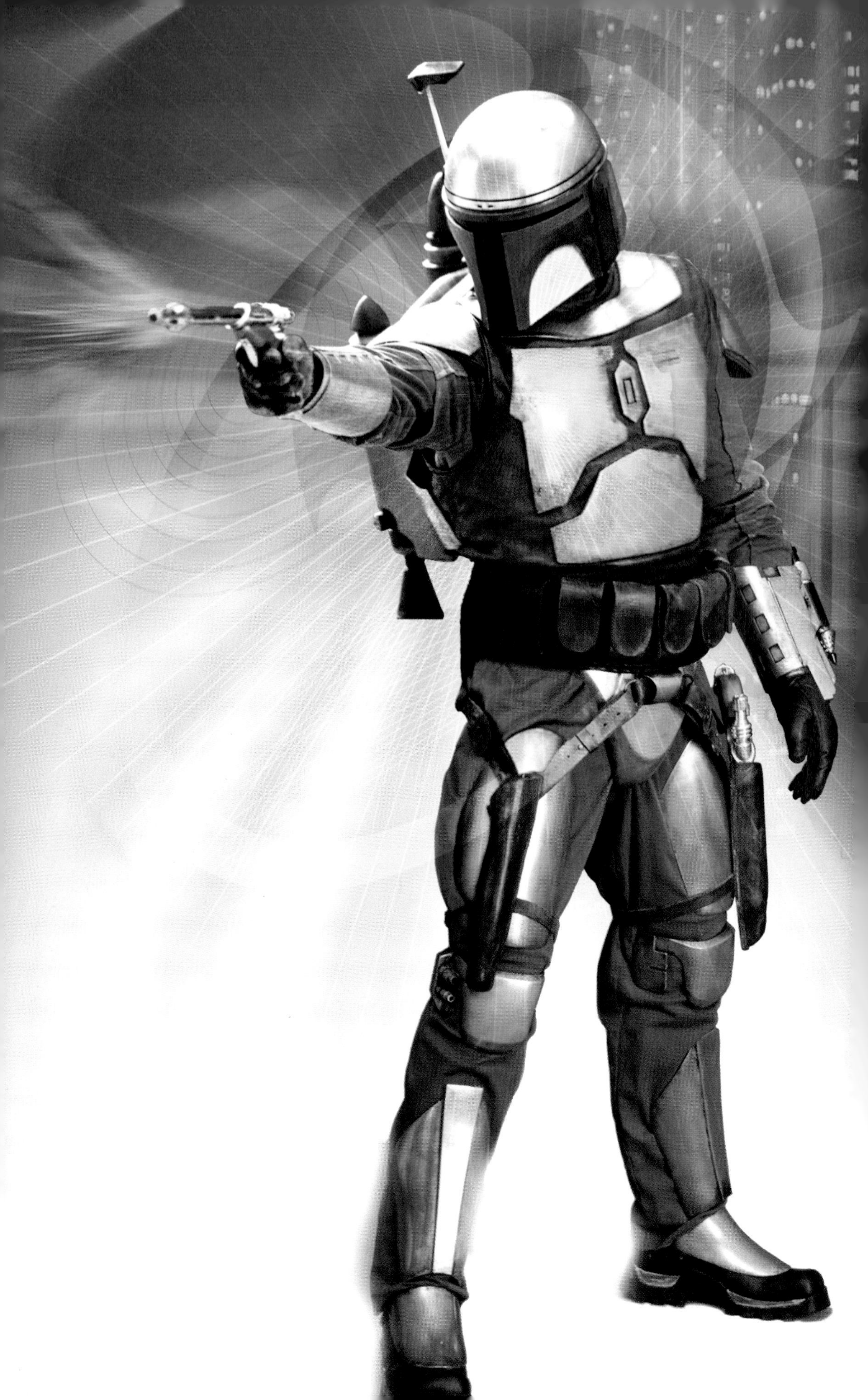

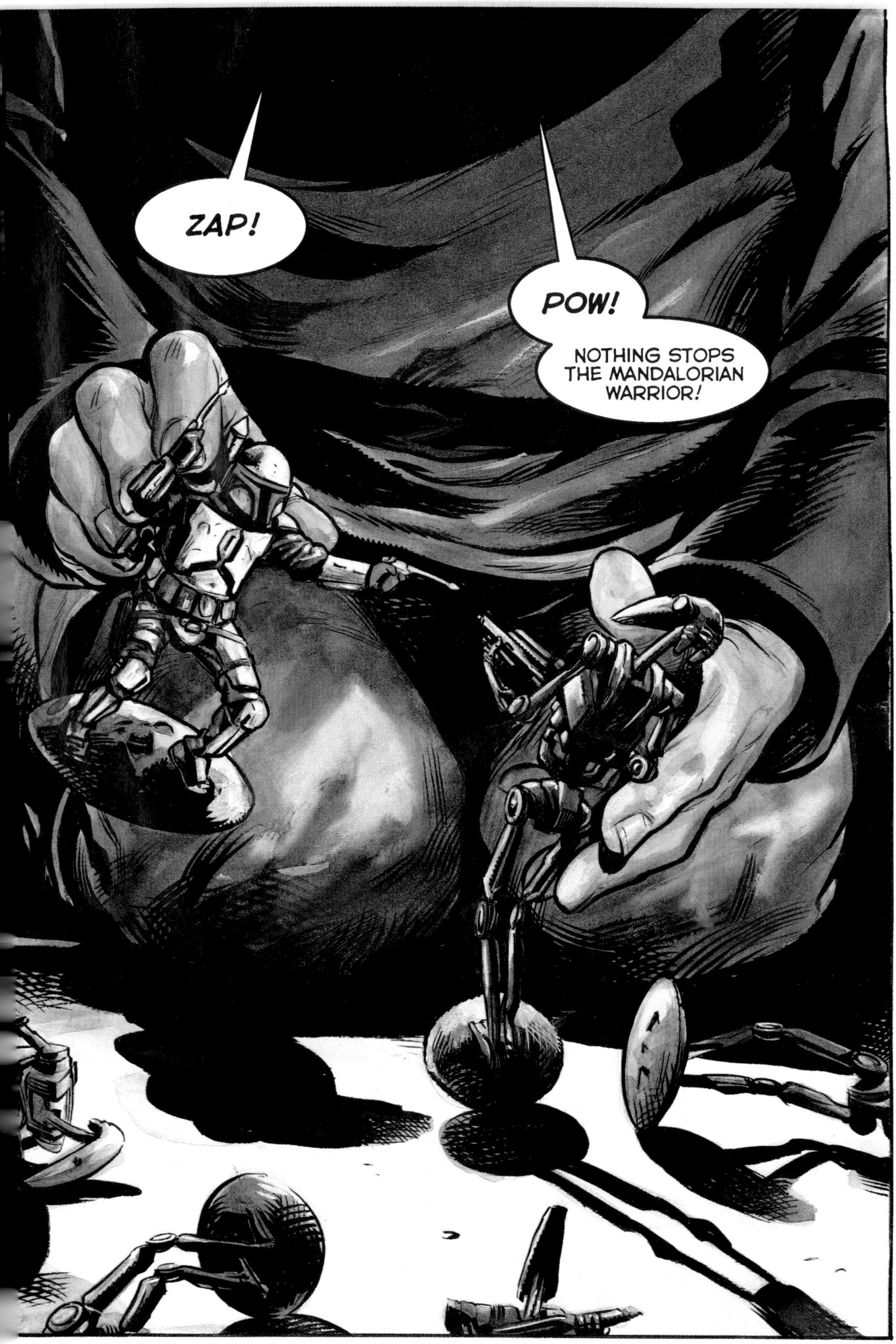
ZAP!
POW!
NOTHING STOPS THE MANDALORIAN WARRIOR!

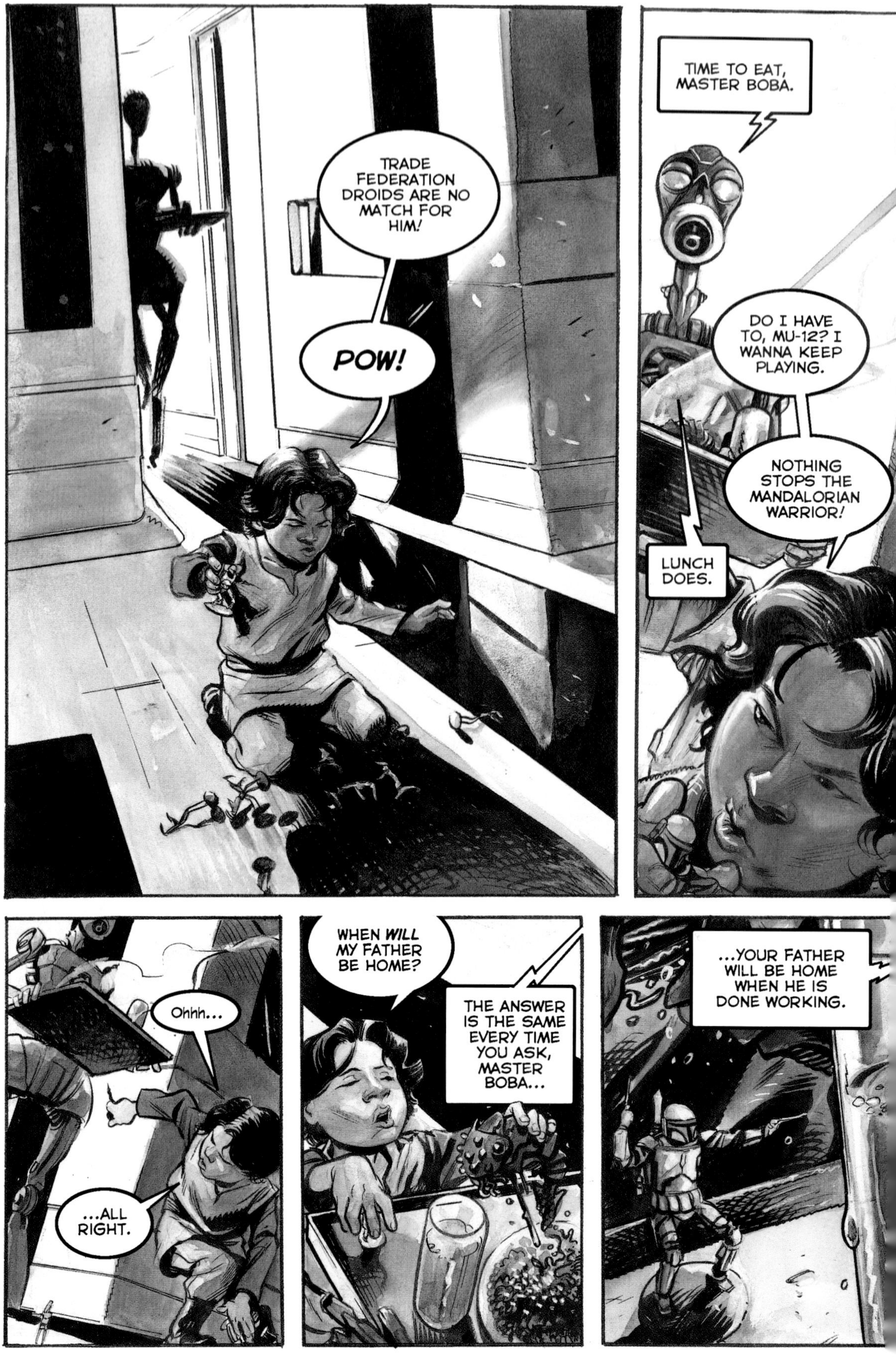
TRADE FEDERATION DROIDS ARE NO MATCH FOR HIM!
POW!
TIME TO EAT, MASTER BOBA.
DO I HAVE TO, MU-12? I WANNA KEEP PLAYING.
NOTHING STOPS THE MANDALORIAN WARRIOR!
LUNCH DOES.
Ohhh...
...ALL RIGHT.
WHEN WILL MY FATHER BE HOME?
THE ANSWER IS THE SAME EVERY TIME YOU ASK, MASTER BOBA...
...YOUR FATHER WILL BE HOME WHEN HE IS DONE WORKING.

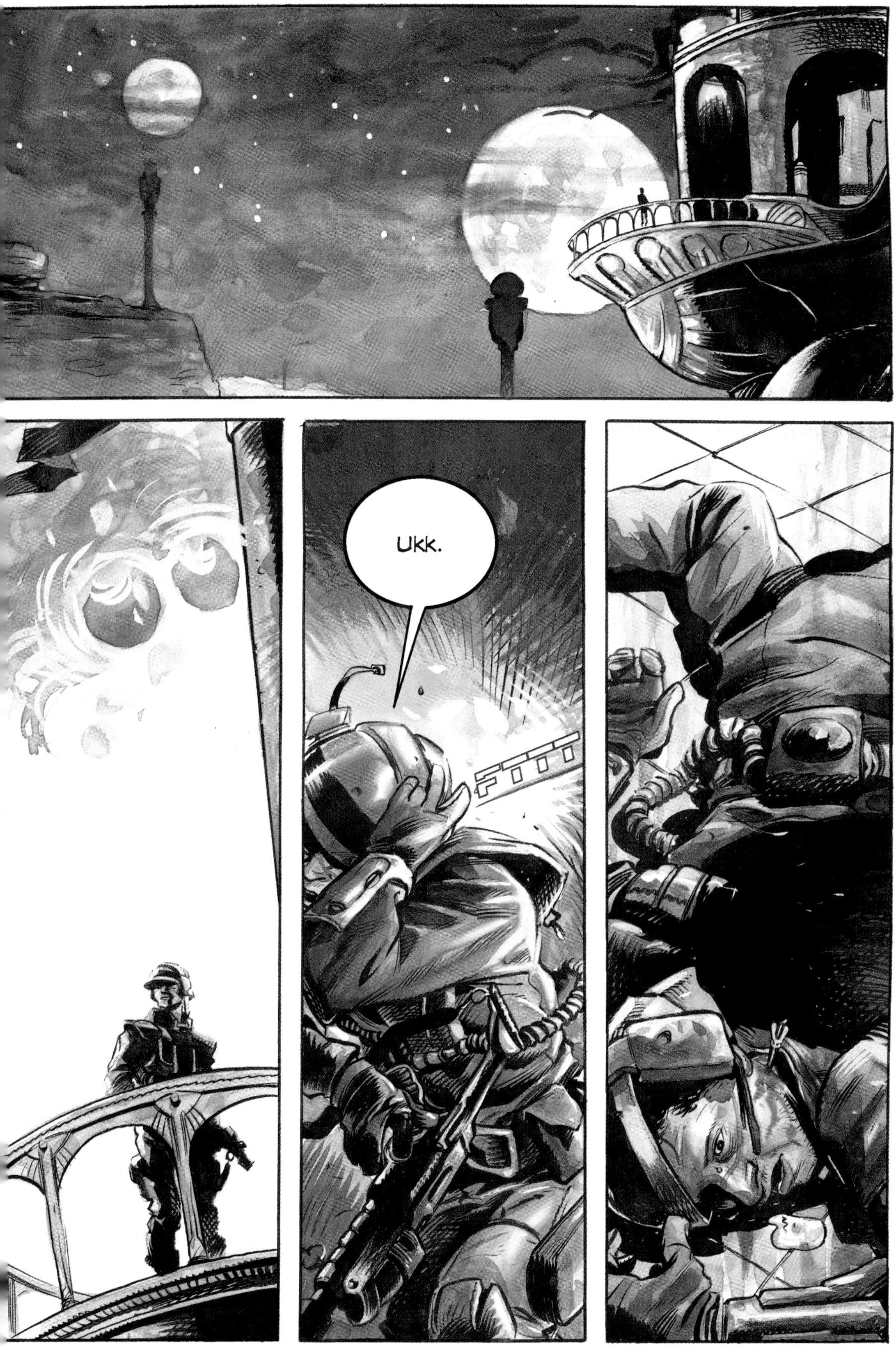
UKK.
FTTT

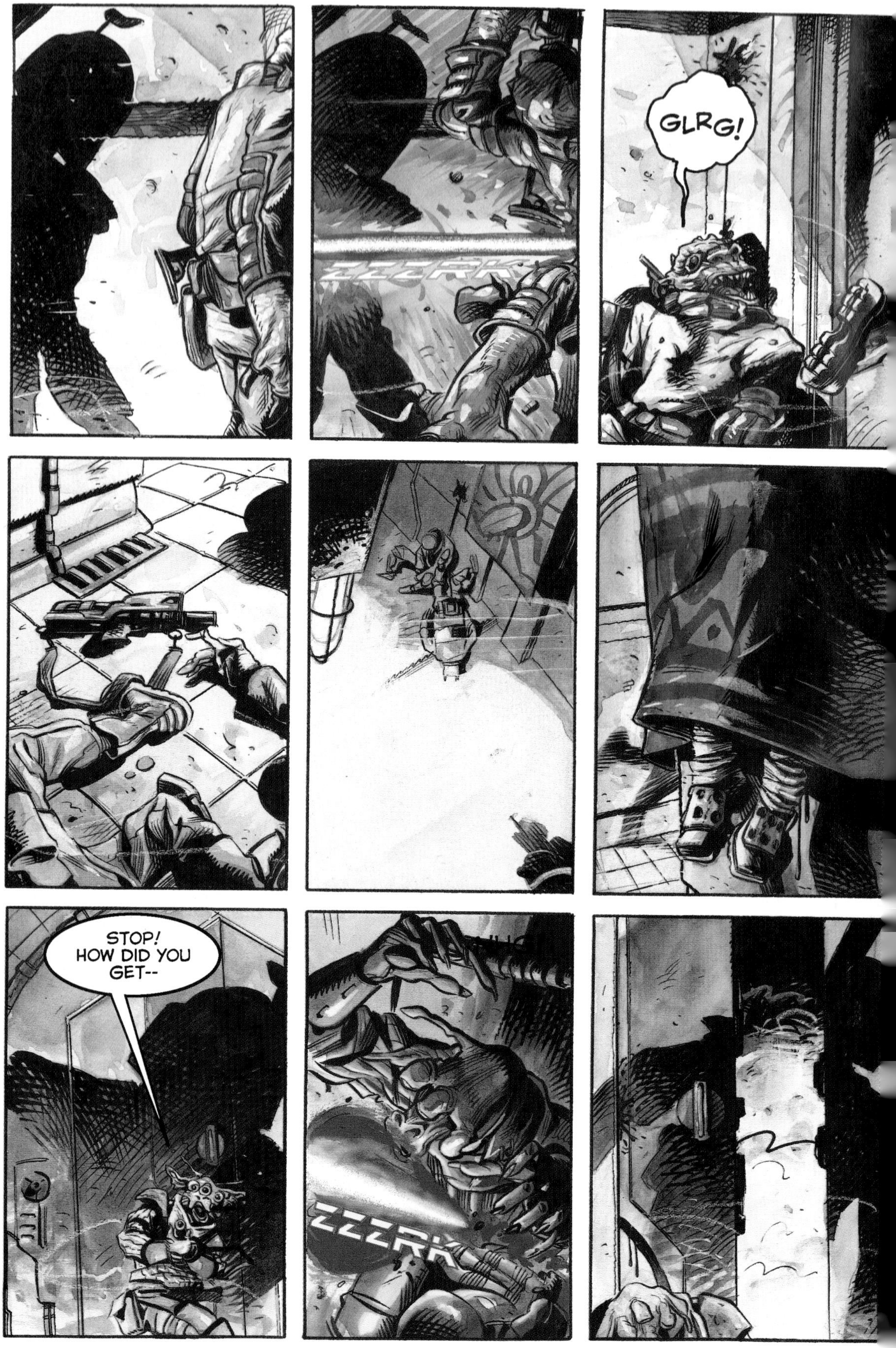
ZZZRK
GLRG!
STOP! HOW DID YOU GET--
ZZZRK

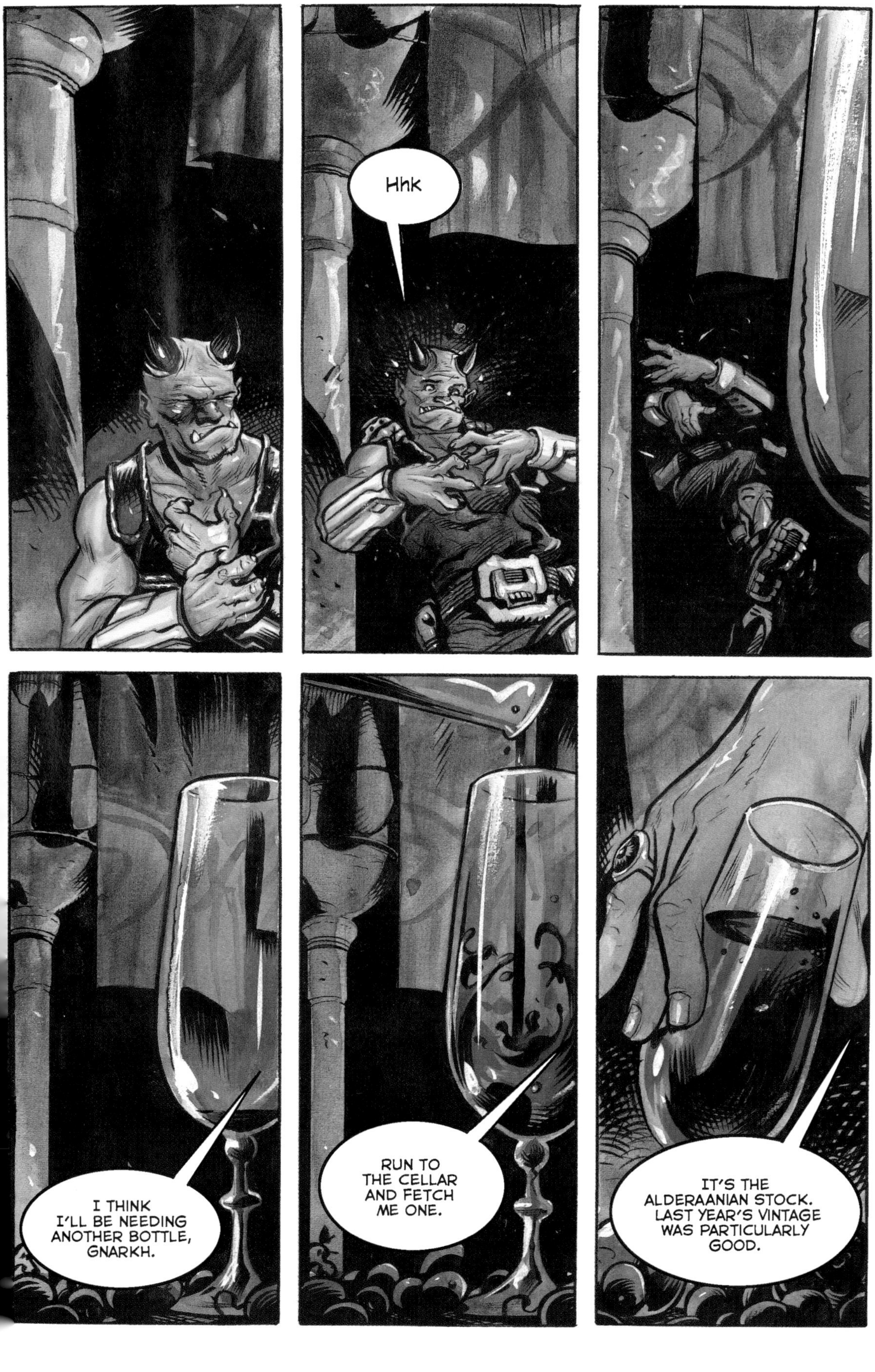
Hhk
I THINK I'LL BE NEEDING ANOTHER BOTTLE, GNARKH.
RUN TO THE CELLAR AND FETCH ME ONE.
IT'S THE ALDERAANIAN STOCK. LAST YEAR'S VINTAGE WAS PARTICULARLY GOOD.

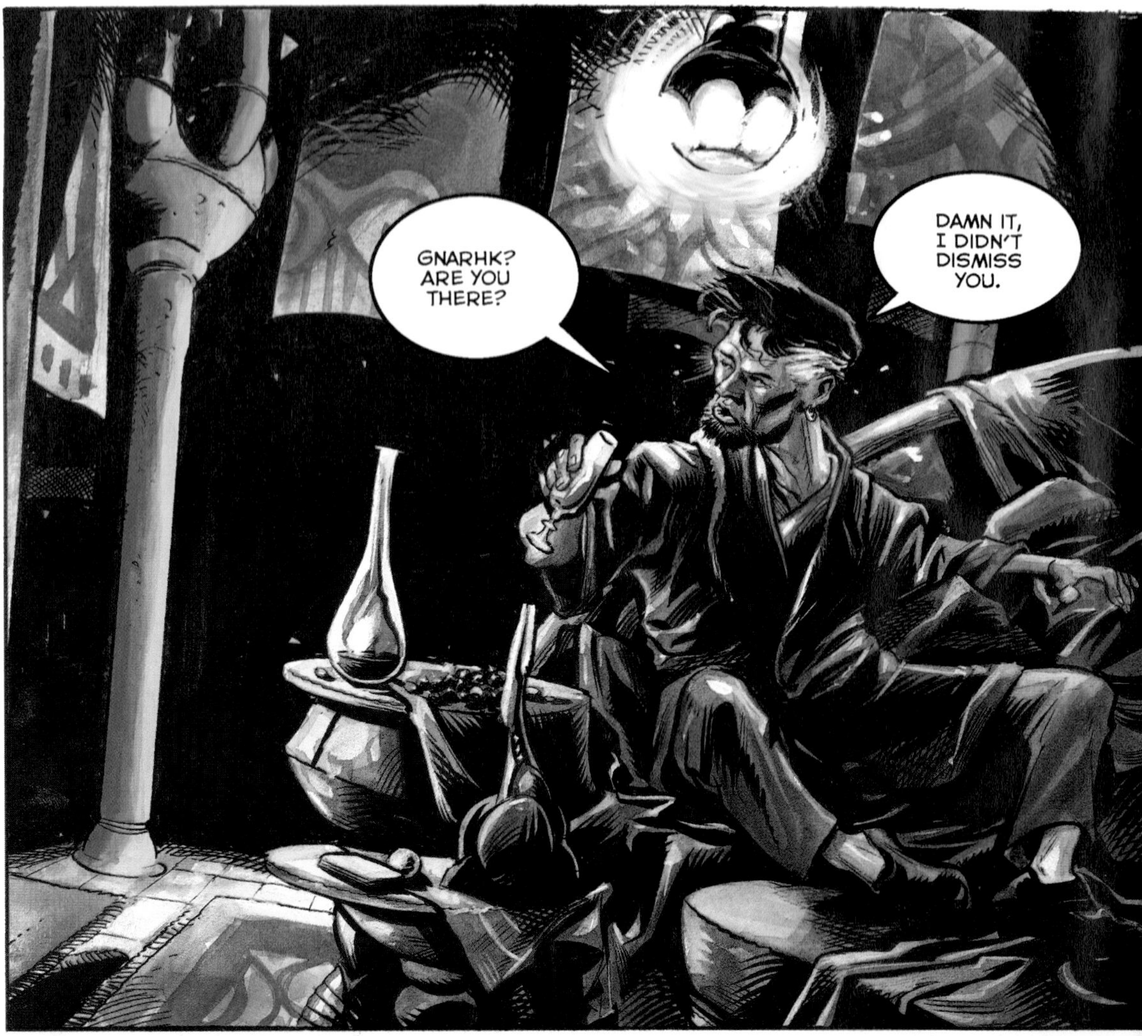
GNARHK? ARE YOU THERE?
DAMN IT, I DIDN'T DISMISS YOU.

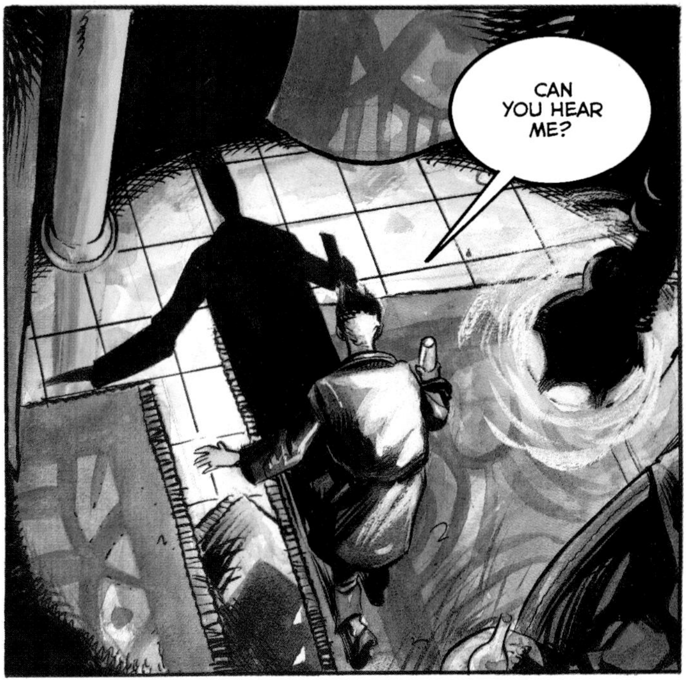
CAN YOU HEAR ME?

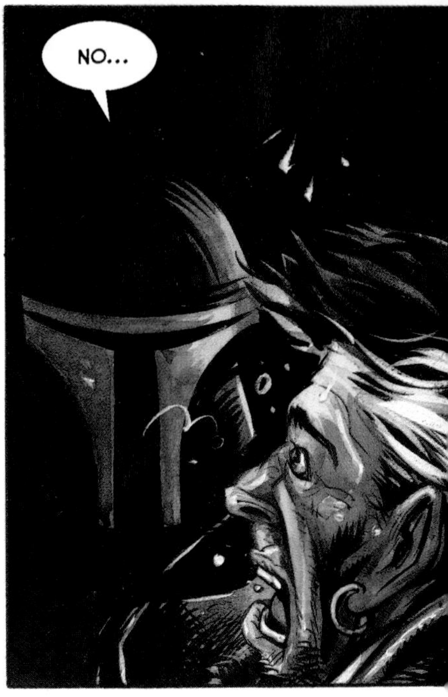
NO...

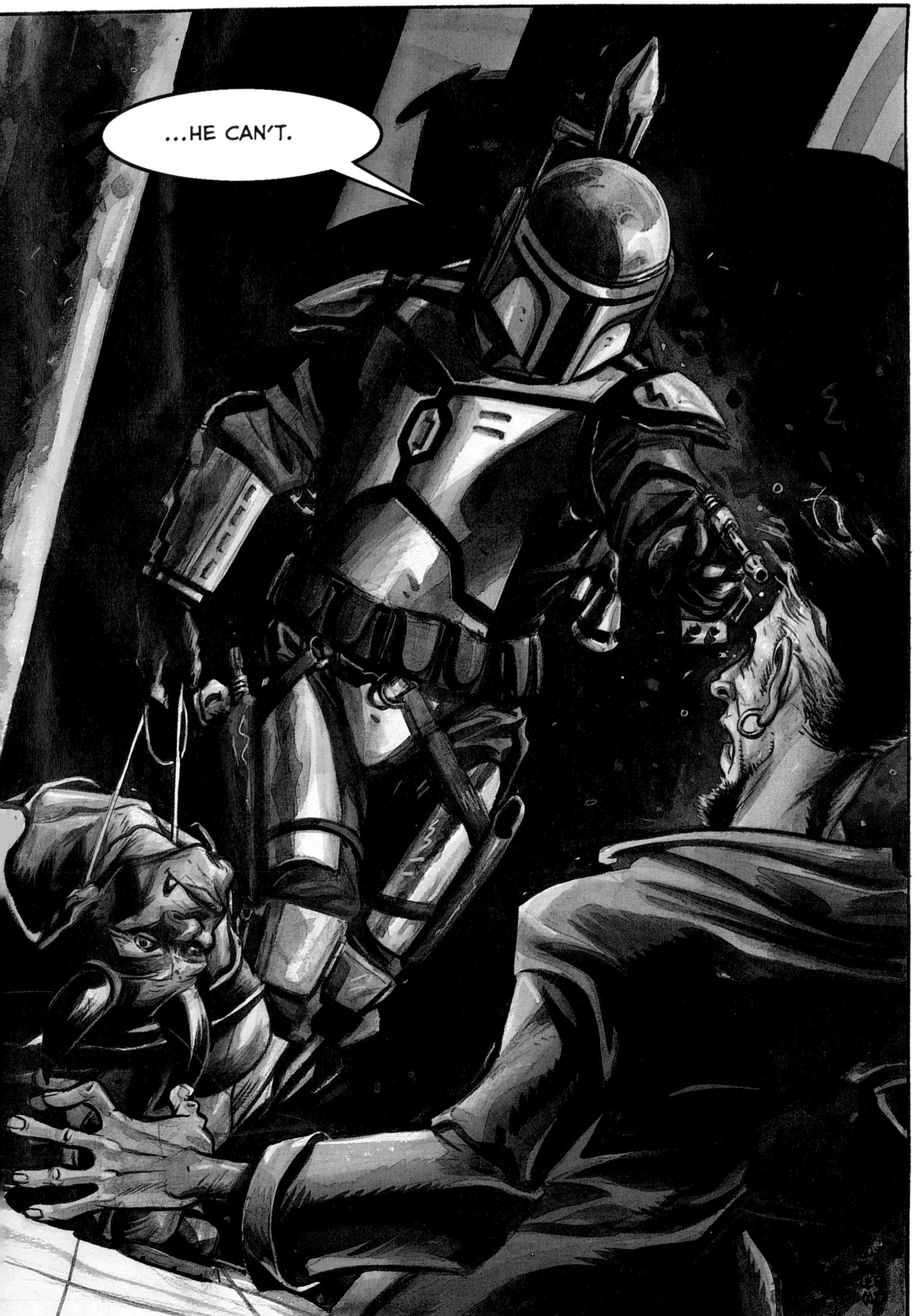
...HE CAN'T.

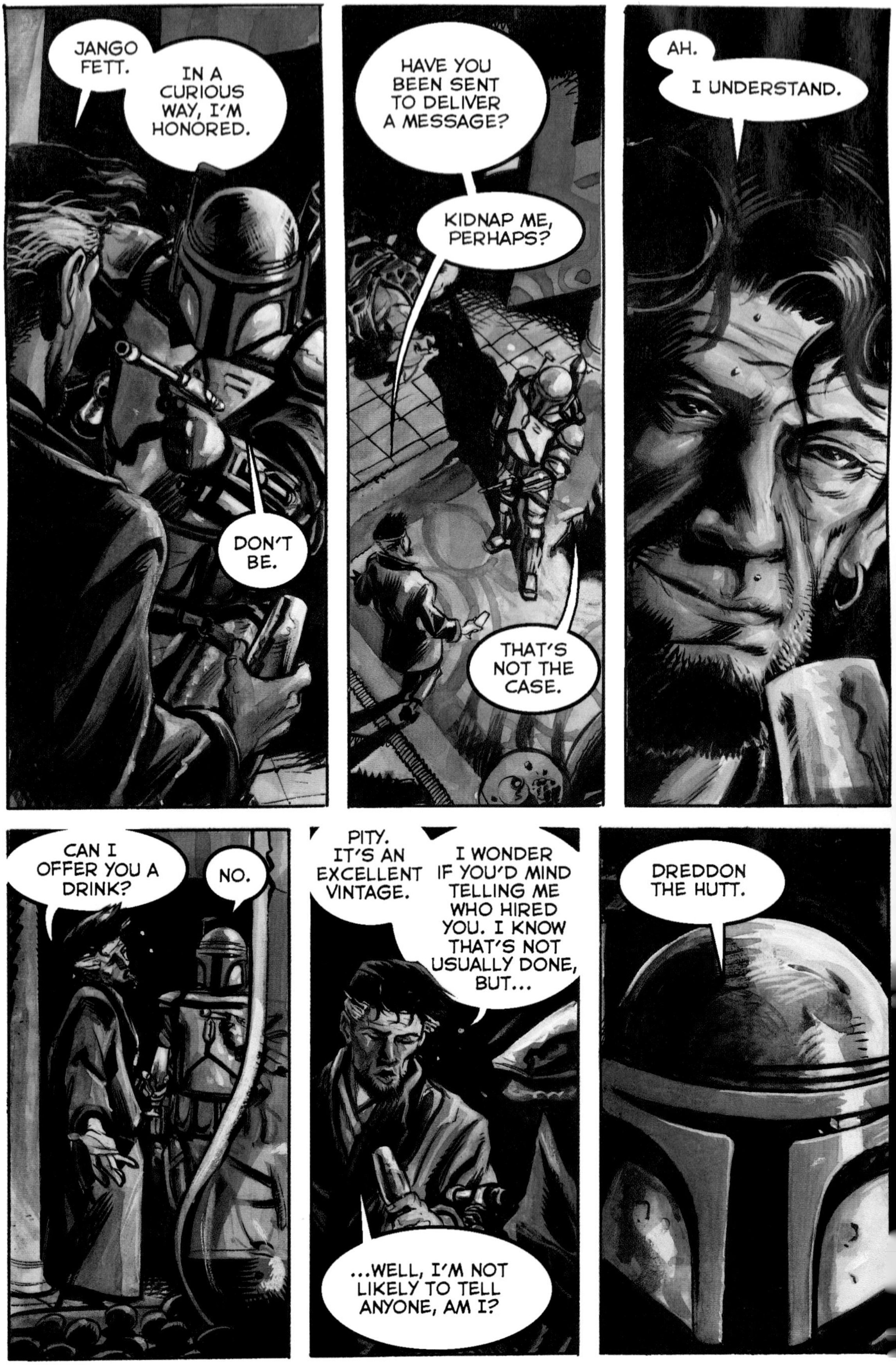
JANGO FETT.
IN A CURIOUS WAY, I'M HONORED.
DON'T BE.
HAVE YOU BEEN SENT TO DELIVER A MESSAGE?
KIDNAP ME, PERHAPS?
THAT'S NOT THE CASE.
AH.
I UNDERSTAND.
CAN I OFFER YOU A DRINK?
NO.
PITY. IT'S AN EXCELLENT VINTAGE.
I WONDER IF YOU'D MIND TELLING ME WHO HIRED YOU. I KNOW THAT'S NOT USUALLY DONE, BUT...
...WELL, I'M NOT LIKELY TO TELL ANYONE, AM I?
DREDDON THE HUTT.

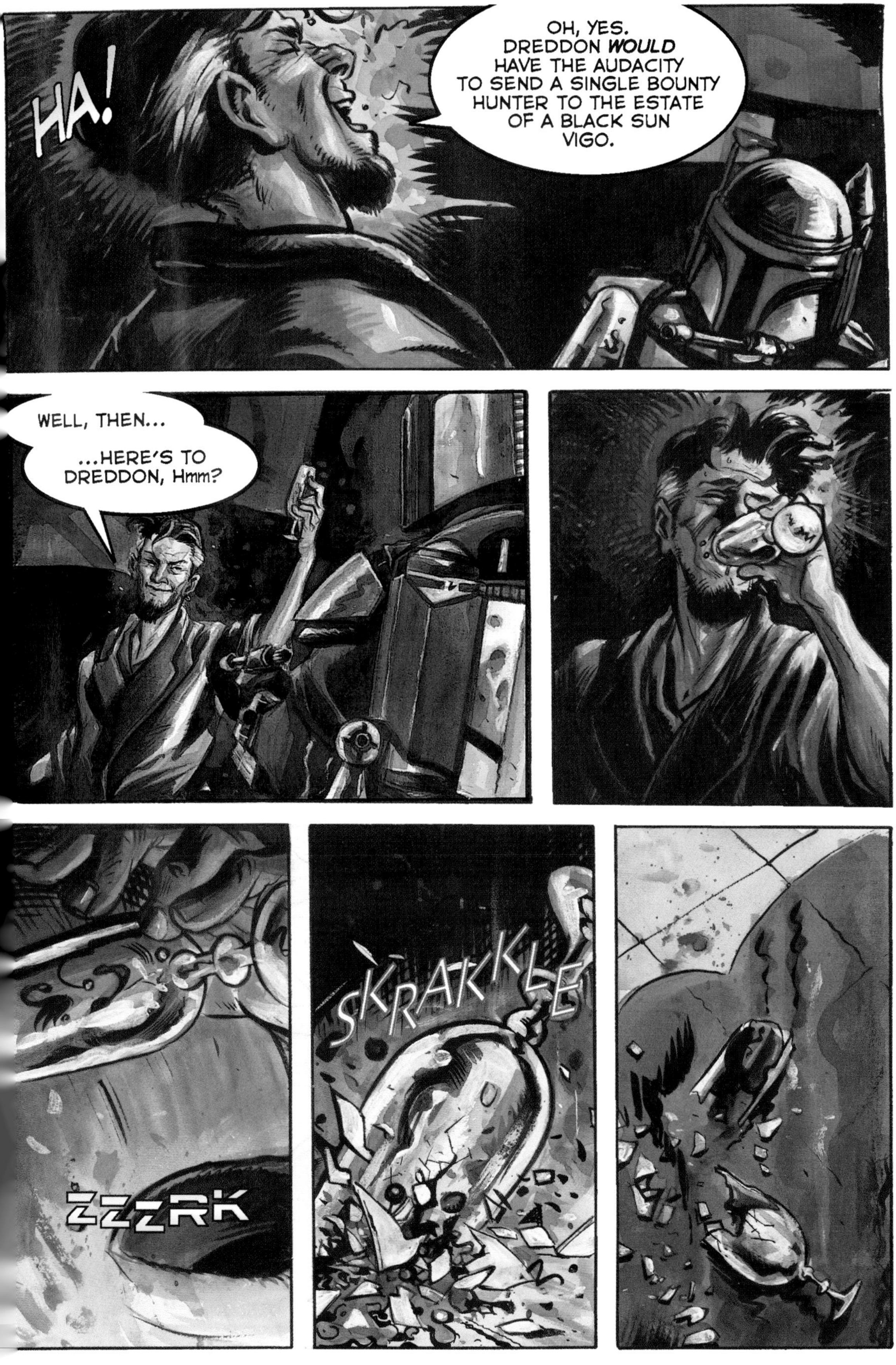
HA!
OH, YES. DREDDON *WOULD* HAVE THE AUDACITY TO SEND A SINGLE BOUNTY HUNTER TO THE ESTATE OF A BLACK SUN VIGO.
WELL, THEN...
...HERE'S TO DREDDON, Hmm?
ZZZRK
SKRAKKLE

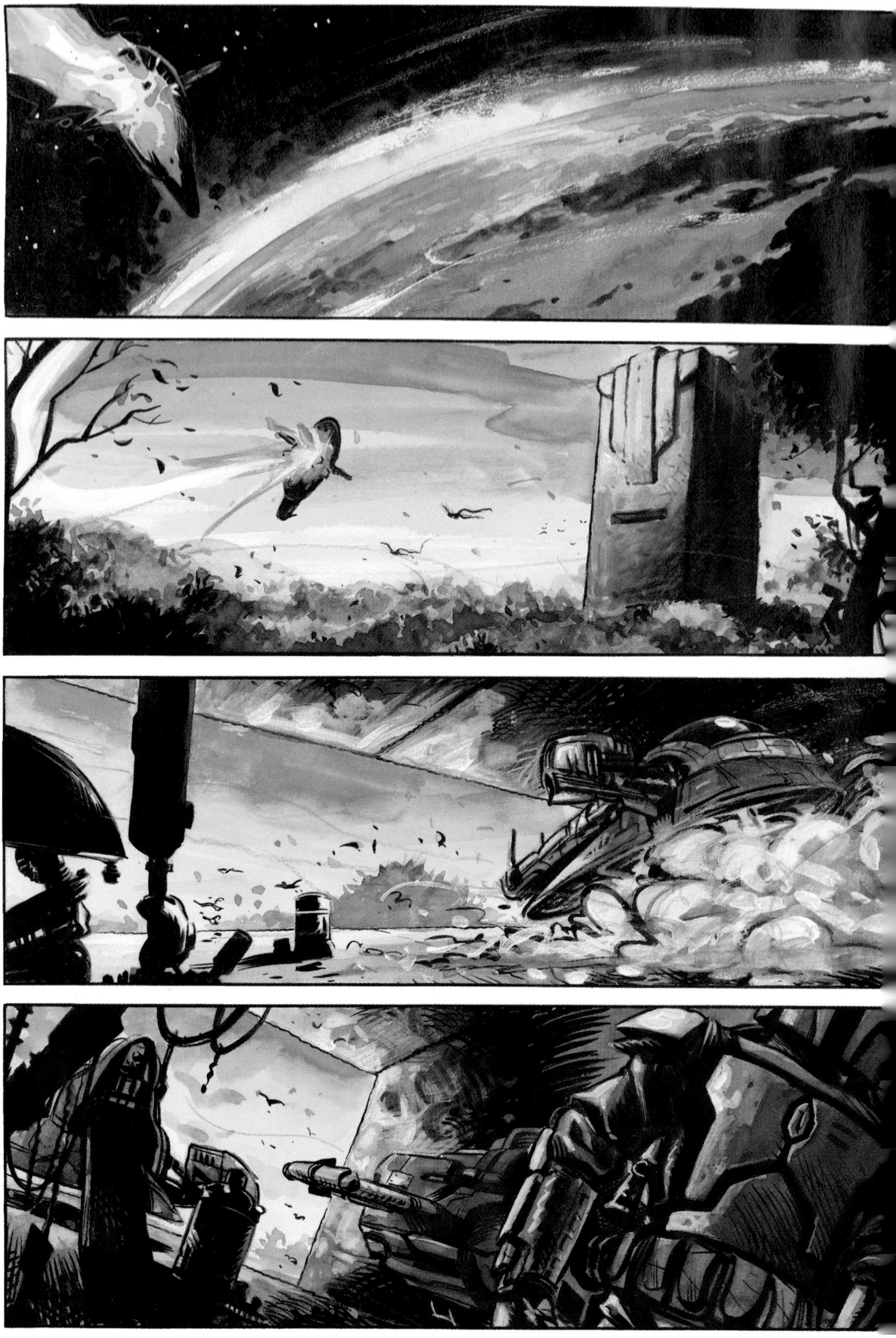

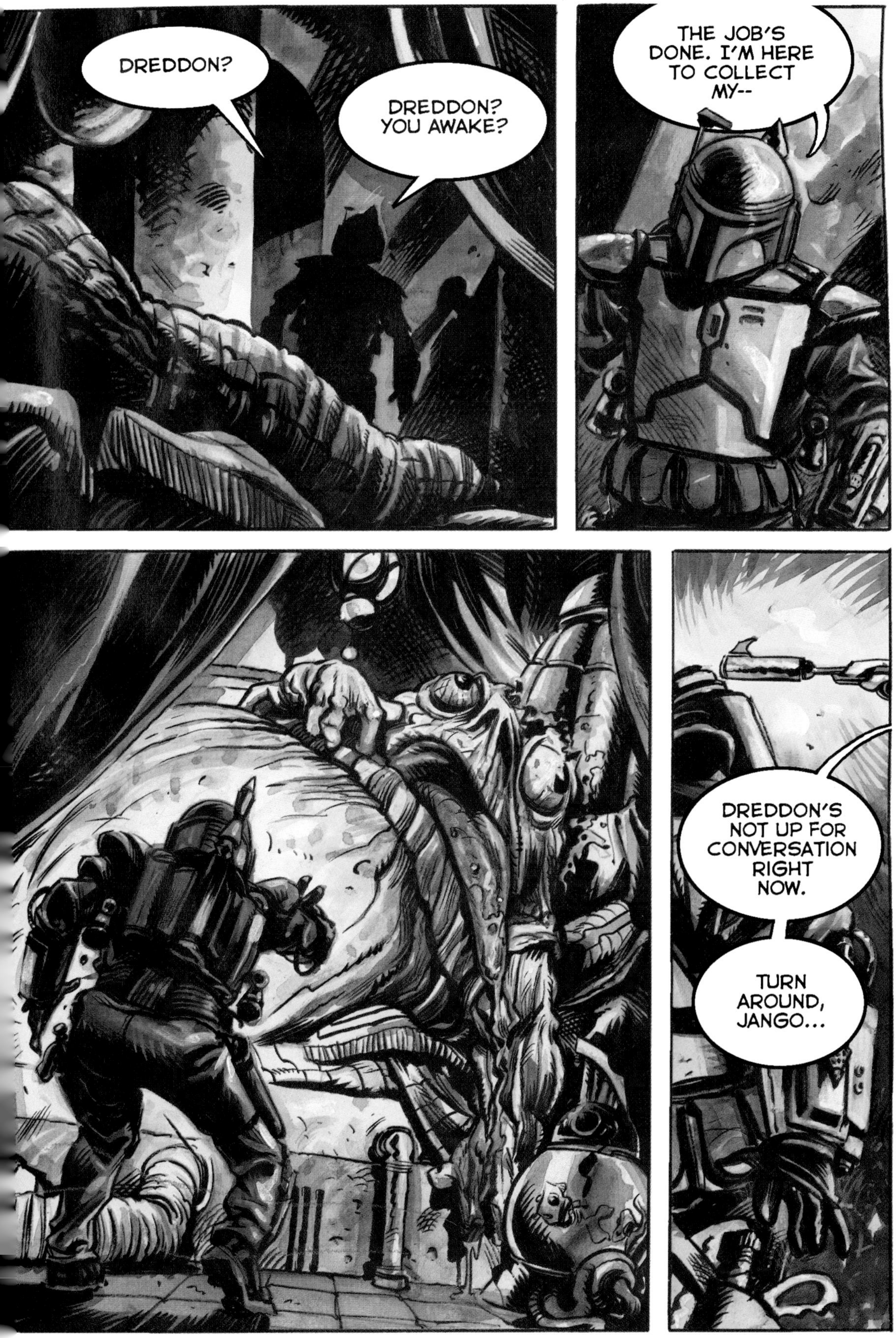
DREDDON?
DREDDON? YOU AWAKE?
THE JOB'S DONE. I'M HERE TO COLLECT MY--
DREDDON'S NOT UP FOR CONVERSATION RIGHT NOW.
TURN AROUND, JANGO...

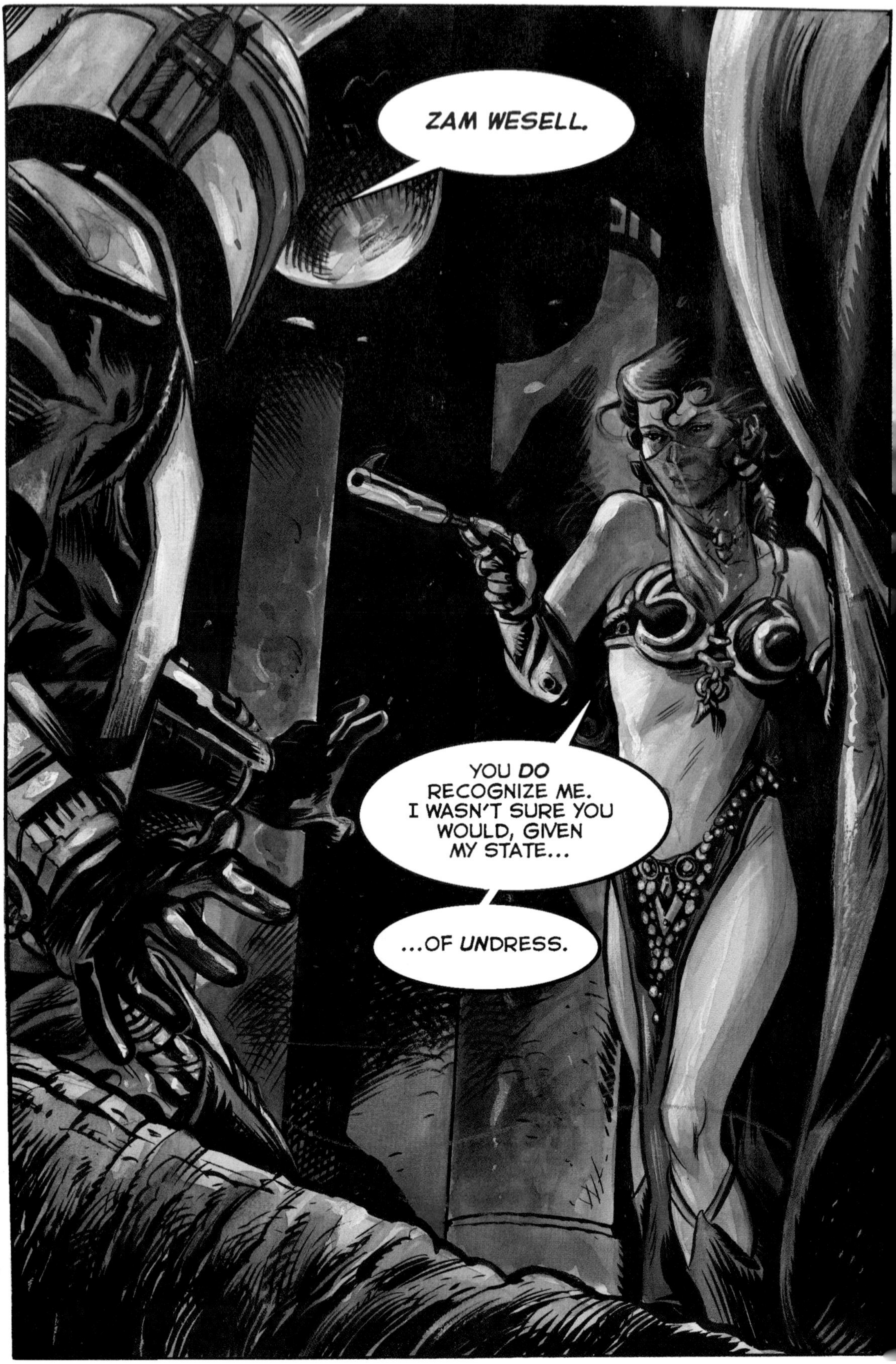
ZAM WESELL.
YOU DO RECOGNIZE ME. I WASN'T SURE YOU WOULD, GIVEN MY STATE...
...OF UNDRESS.

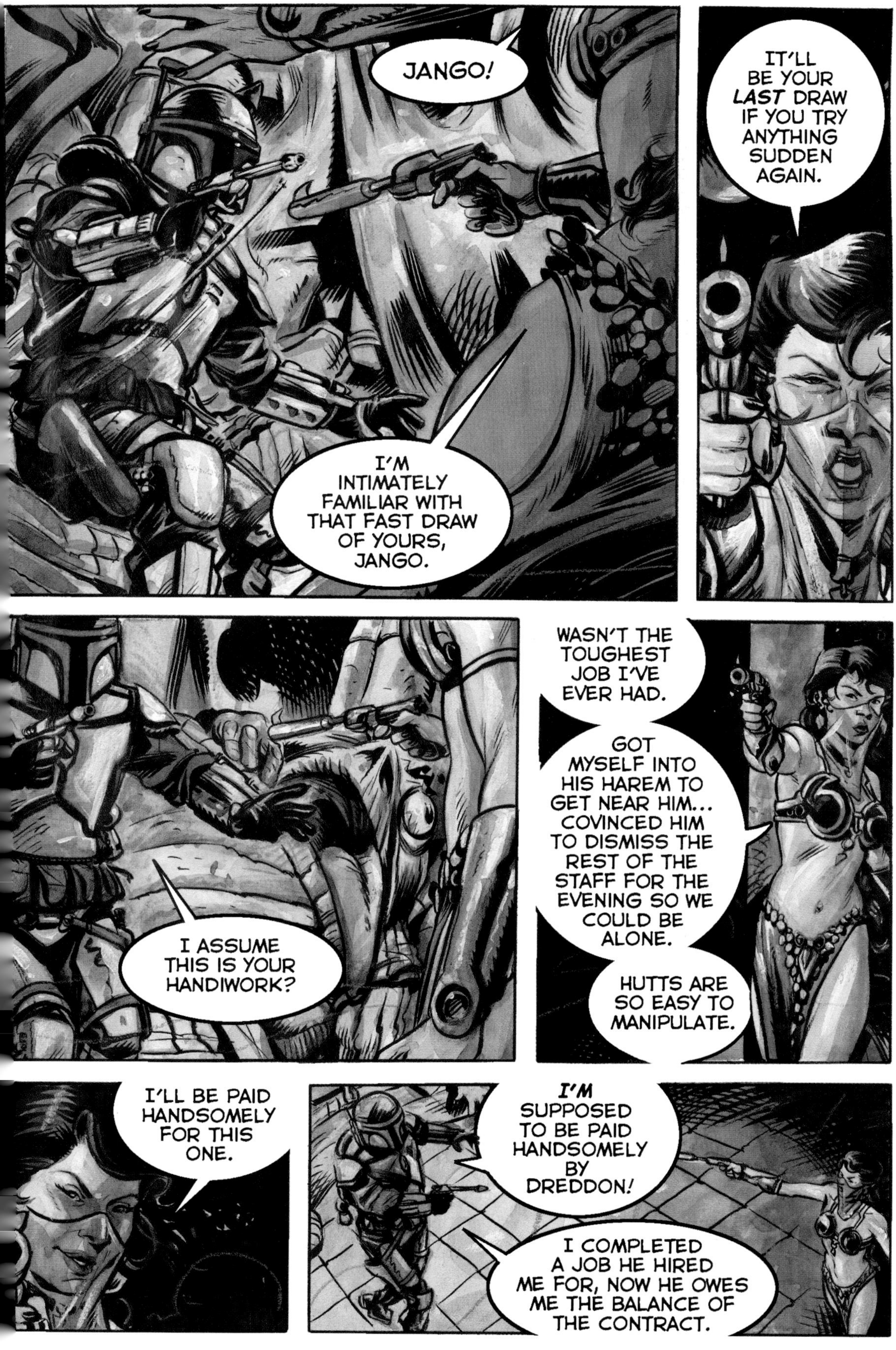

JANGO!
I'M INTIMATELY FAMILIAR WITH THAT FAST DRAW OF YOURS, JANGO.
IT'LL BE YOUR *LAST* DRAW IF YOU TRY ANYTHING SUDDEN AGAIN.
I ASSUME THIS IS YOUR HANDIWORK?
WASN'T THE TOUGHEST JOB I'VE EVER HAD.
GOT MYSELF INTO HIS HAREM TO GET NEAR HIM... COVINCED HIM TO DISMISS THE REST OF THE STAFF FOR THE EVENING SO WE COULD BE ALONE.
HUTTS ARE SO EASY TO MANIPULATE.
I'LL BE PAID HANDSOMELY FOR THIS ONE.
I'M SUPPOSED TO BE PAID HANDSOMELY BY DREDDON!
I COMPLETED A JOB HE HIRED ME FOR, NOW HE OWES ME THE BALANCE OF THE CONTRACT.

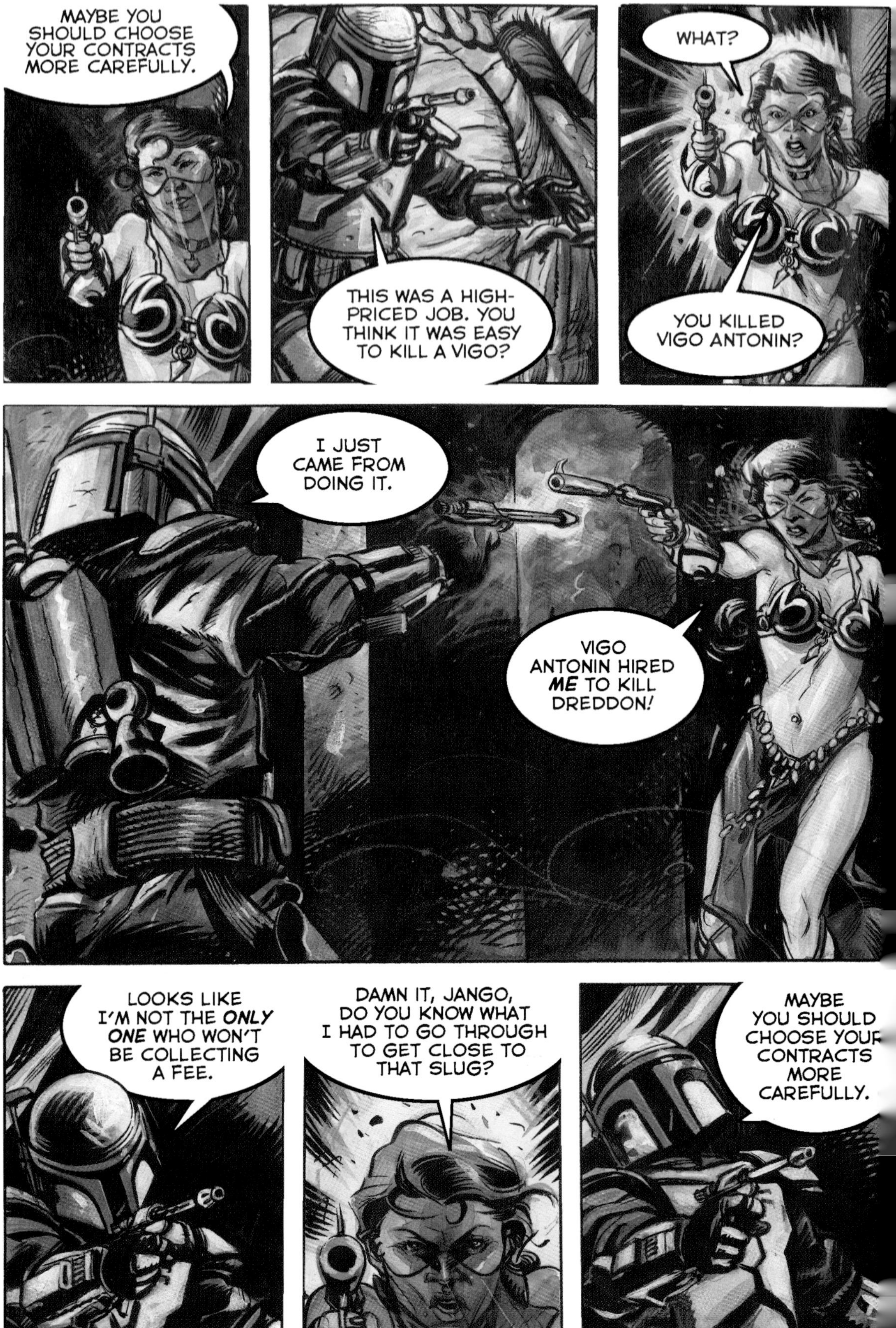
MAYBE YOU SHOULD CHOOSE YOUR CONTRACTS MORE CAREFULLY.
THIS WAS A HIGH-PRICED JOB. YOU THINK IT WAS EASY TO KILL A VIGO?
WHAT?
YOU KILLED VIGO ANTONIN?
I JUST CAME FROM DOING IT.
VIGO ANTONIN HIRED *ME* TO KILL DREDDON!
LOOKS LIKE I'M NOT THE *ONLY ONE* WHO WON'T BE COLLECTING A FEE.
DAMN IT, JANGO, DO YOU KNOW WHAT I HAD TO GO THROUGH TO GET CLOSE TO THAT SLUG?
MAYBE YOU SHOULD CHOOSE YOUR CONTRACTS MORE CAREFULLY.

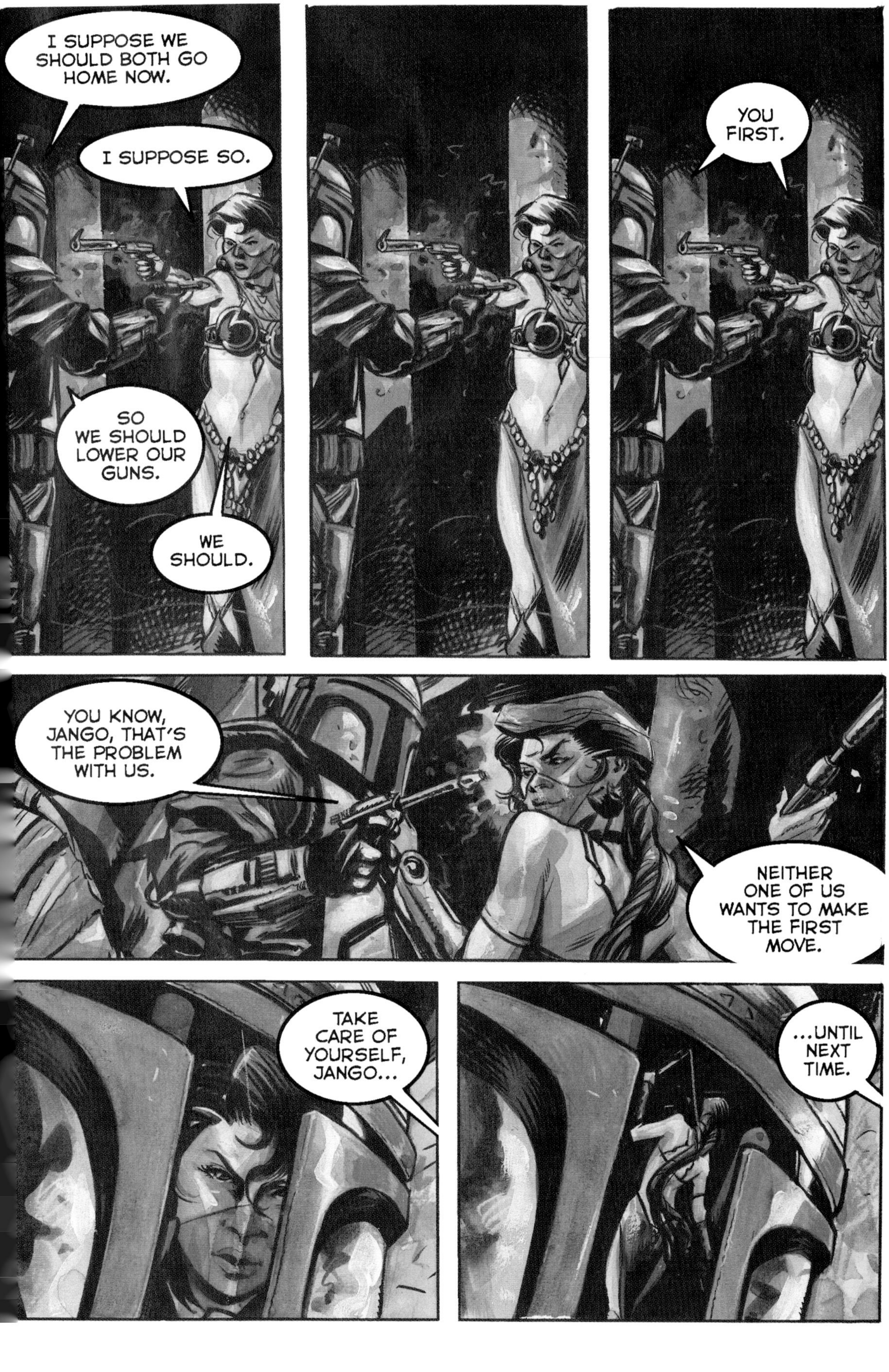
I SUPPOSE WE SHOULD BOTH GO HOME NOW.
I SUPPOSE SO.
SO WE SHOULD LOWER OUR GUNS.
WE SHOULD.
YOU FIRST.
YOU KNOW, JANGO, THAT'S THE PROBLEM WITH US.
NEITHER ONE OF US WANTS TO MAKE THE FIRST MOVE.
TAKE CARE OF YOURSELF, JANGO...
...UNTIL NEXT TIME.

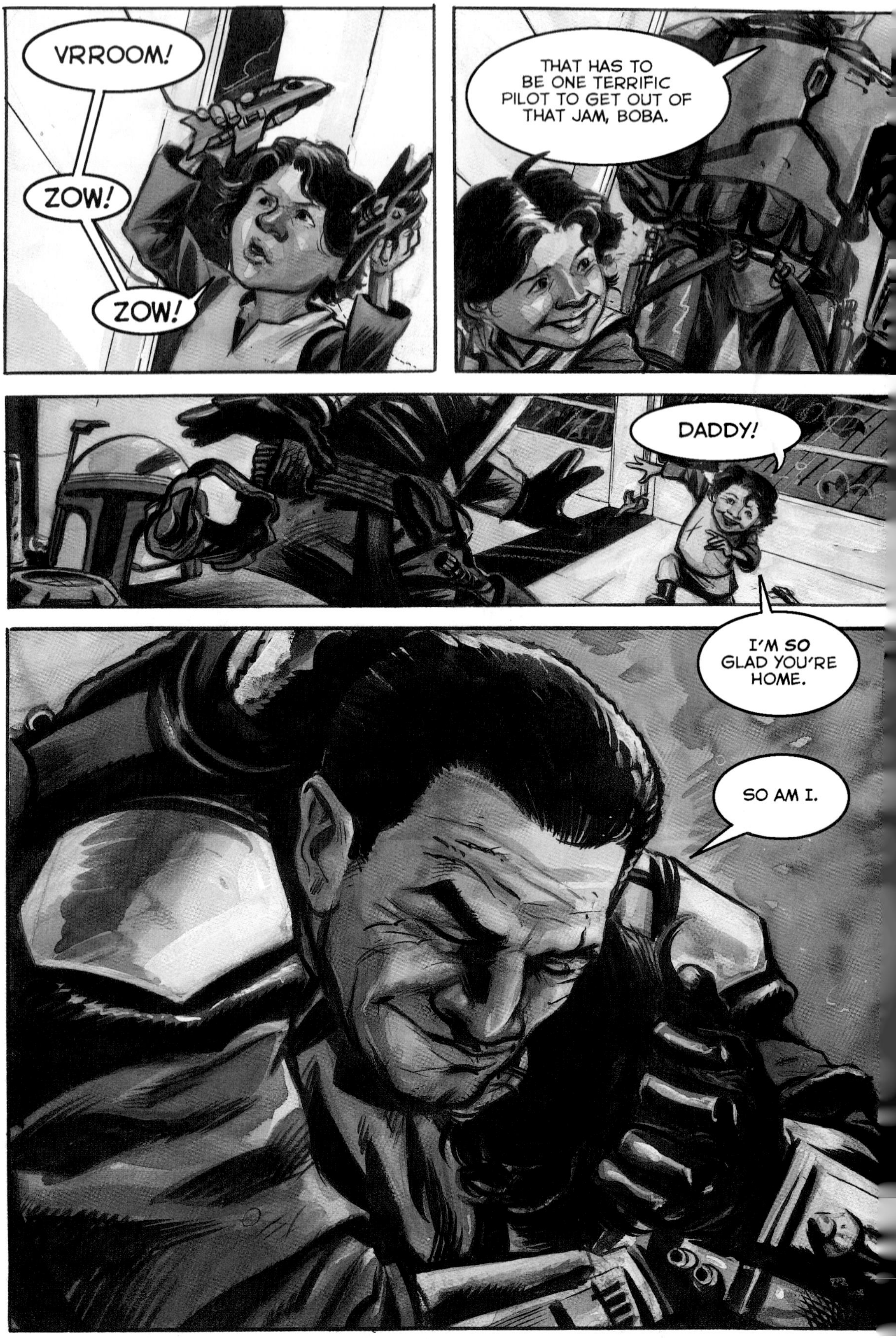
VRROOM!
ZOW!
ZOW!
THAT HAS TO BE ONE TERRIFIC PILOT TO GET OUT OF THAT JAM, BOBA.
DADDY!
I'M SO GLAD YOU'RE HOME.
SO AM I.

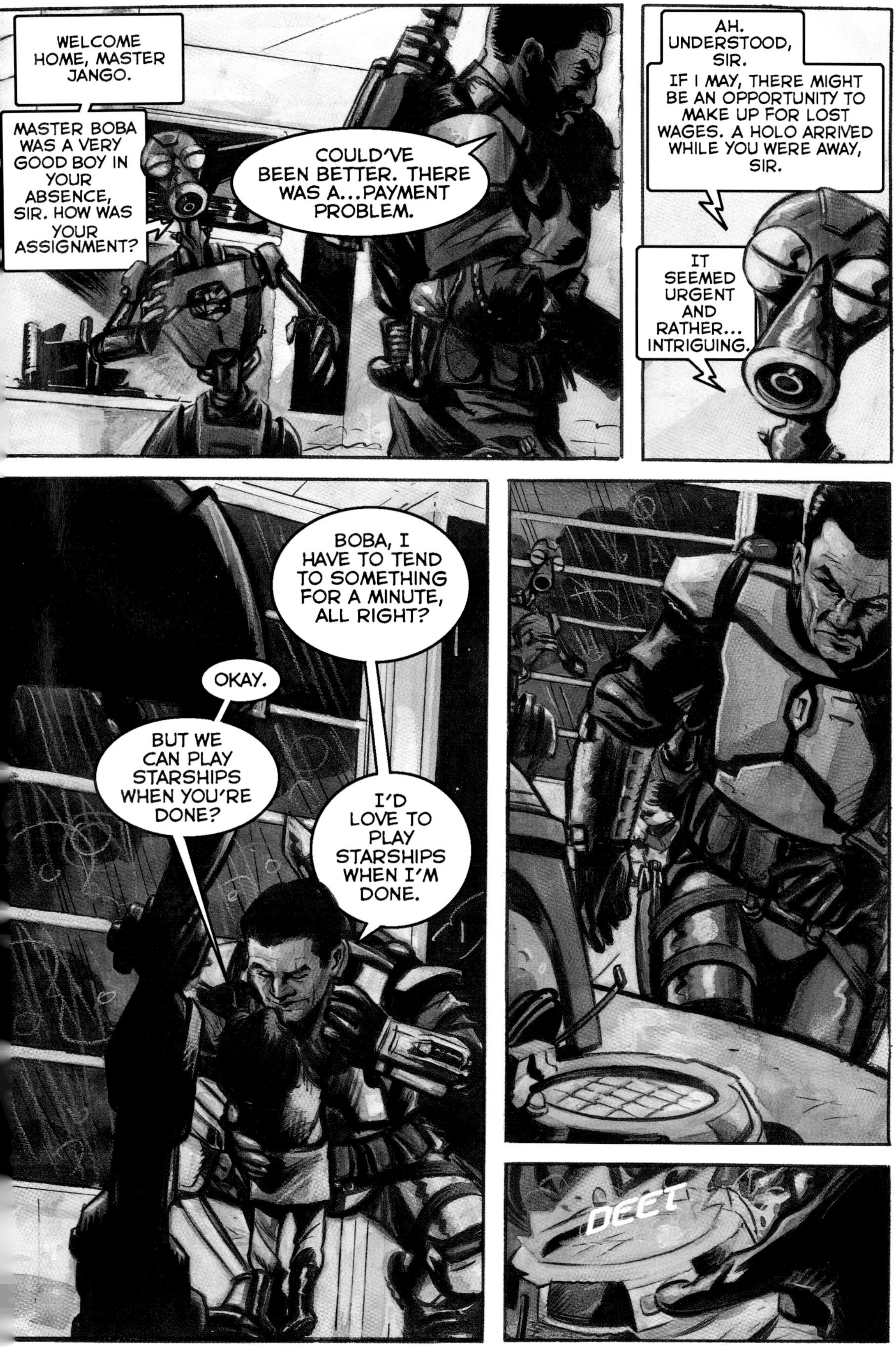
WELCOME HOME, MASTER JANGO.
MASTER BOBA WAS A VERY GOOD BOY IN YOUR ABSENCE, SIR. HOW WAS YOUR ASSIGNMENT?
COULD'VE BEEN BETTER. THERE WAS A...PAYMENT PROBLEM.
AH. UNDERSTOOD, SIR.
IF I MAY, THERE MIGHT BE AN OPPORTUNITY TO MAKE UP FOR LOST WAGES. A HOLO ARRIVED WHILE YOU WERE AWAY, SIR.
IT SEEMED URGENT AND RATHER... INTRIGUING.
BOBA, I HAVE TO TEND TO SOMETHING FOR A MINUTE, ALL RIGHT?
OKAY.
BUT WE CAN PLAY STARSHIPS WHEN YOU'RE DONE?
I'D LOVE TO PLAY STARSHIPS WHEN I'M DONE.
DEET

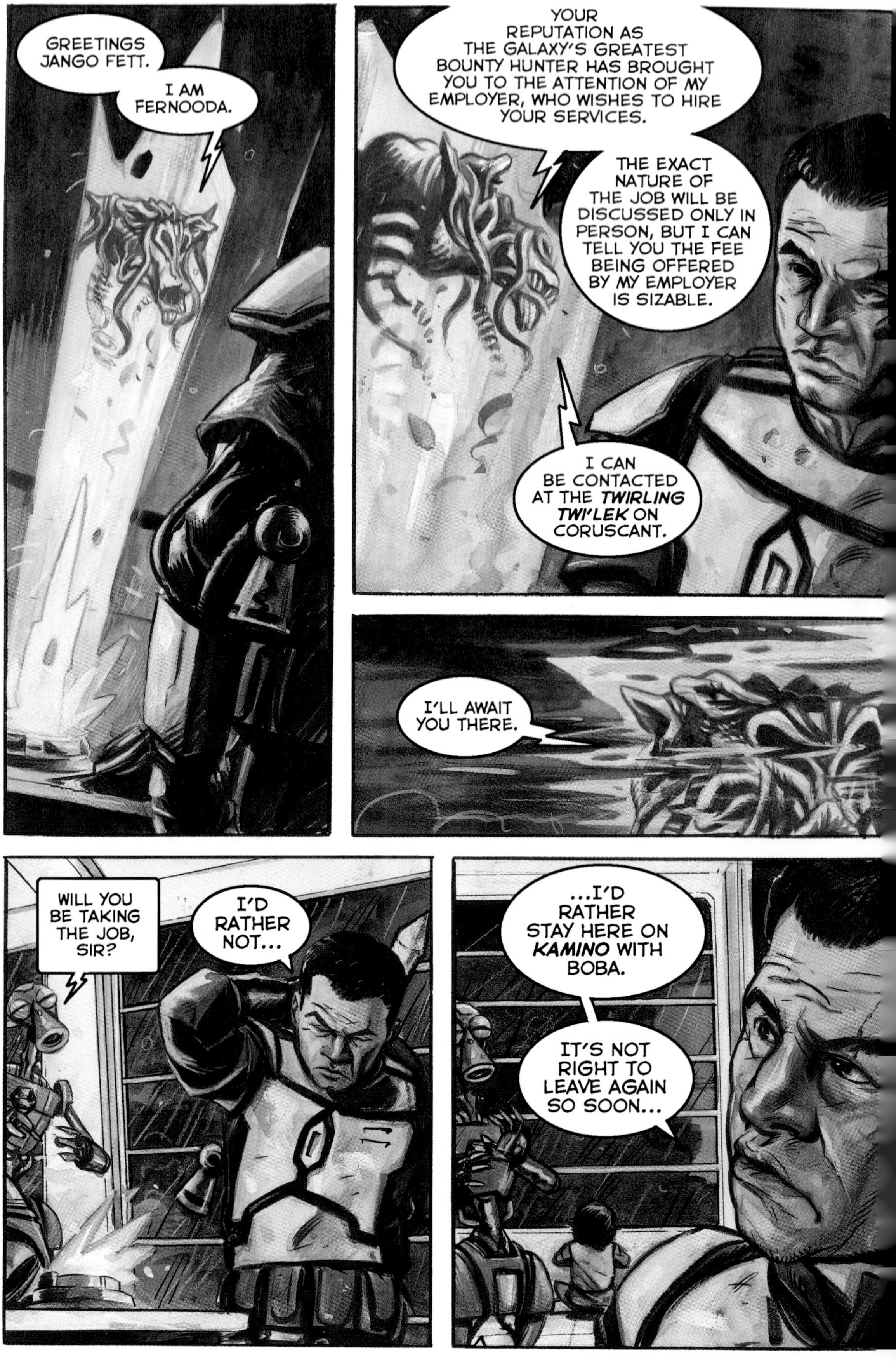
GREETINGS JANGO FETT.
I AM FERNOODA.
YOUR REPUTATION AS THE GALAXY'S GREATEST BOUNTY HUNTER HAS BROUGHT YOU TO THE ATTENTION OF MY EMPLOYER, WHO WISHES TO HIRE YOUR SERVICES.
THE EXACT NATURE OF THE JOB WILL BE DISCUSSED ONLY IN PERSON, BUT I CAN TELL YOU THE FEE BEING OFFERED BY MY EMPLOYER IS SIZABLE.
I CAN BE CONTACTED AT THE *TWIRLING TWI'LEK* ON CORUSCANT.
I'LL AWAIT YOU THERE.
WILL YOU BE TAKING THE JOB, SIR?
I'D RATHER NOT...
...I'D RATHER STAY HERE ON *KAMINO* WITH BOBA.
IT'S NOT RIGHT TO LEAVE AGAIN SO SOON...

...BUT I DO HAVE TO MAKE UP FOR LOST PROFITS ON THE LAST JOB.

BOBA...

...WE NEED TO TALK.

YOU'RE GOING AWAY AGAIN, AREN'T YOU?

YOU JUST GOT HOME BUT YOU'RE GOING AWAY AGAIN.

I...

...YES.

SOMETHING'S COME UP AND I NEED TO TEND TO IT. I'M SORRY, SON. I SHOULDN'T BE GONE LONG.

IT DOESN'T MEAN I LOVE YOU ANY LESS. YOU UNDERSTAND THAT, DON'T YOU?

I UNDERSTAND, BUT...

...DO YOU HAVE TO GO RIGHT NOW?

NO...

"...NOT RIGHT NOW"

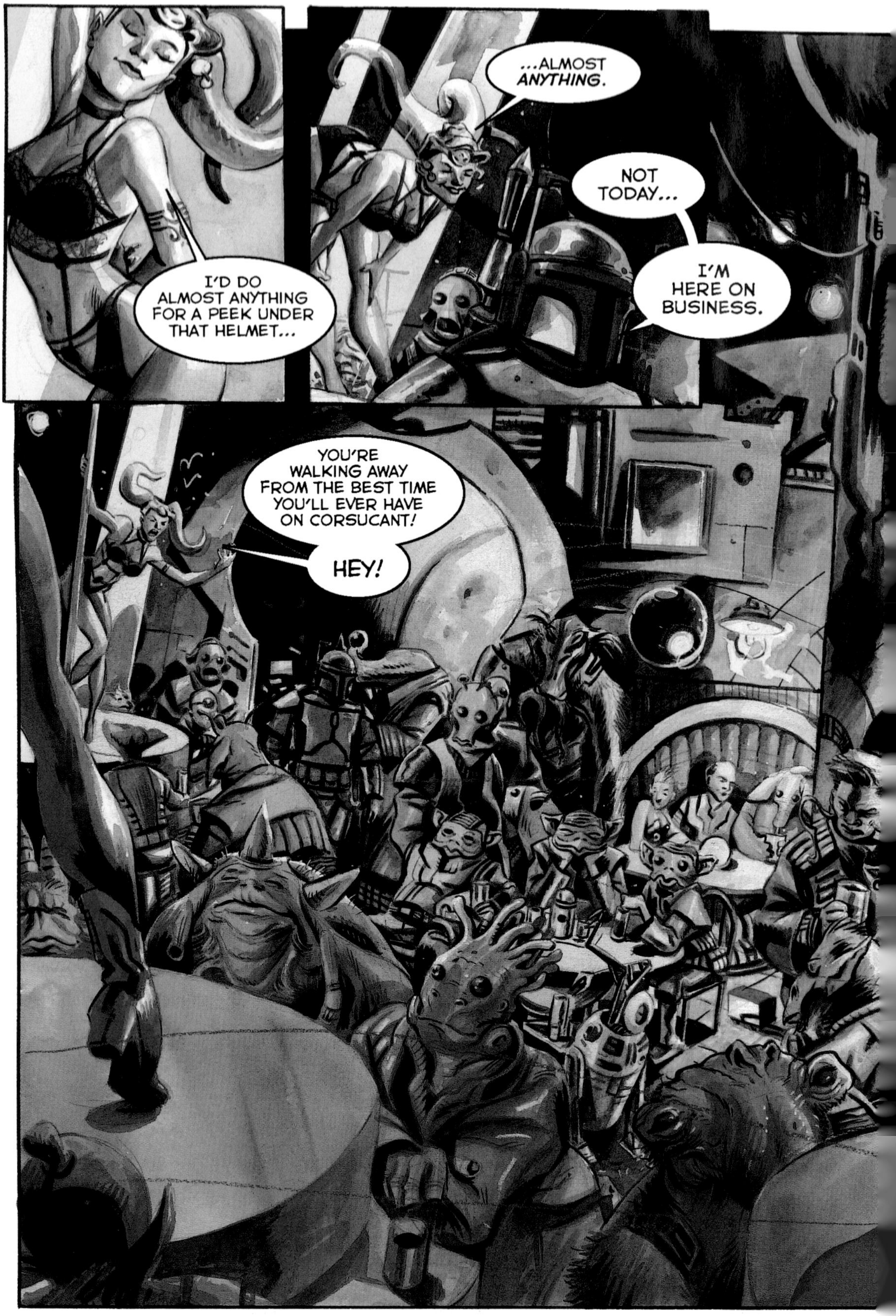
I'D DO ALMOST ANYTHING FOR A PEEK UNDER THAT HELMET...
...ALMOST *ANYTHING*.
NOT TODAY...
I'M HERE ON BUSINESS.
YOU'RE WALKING AWAY FROM THE BEST TIME YOU'LL EVER HAVE ON CORSUCANT!
HEY!

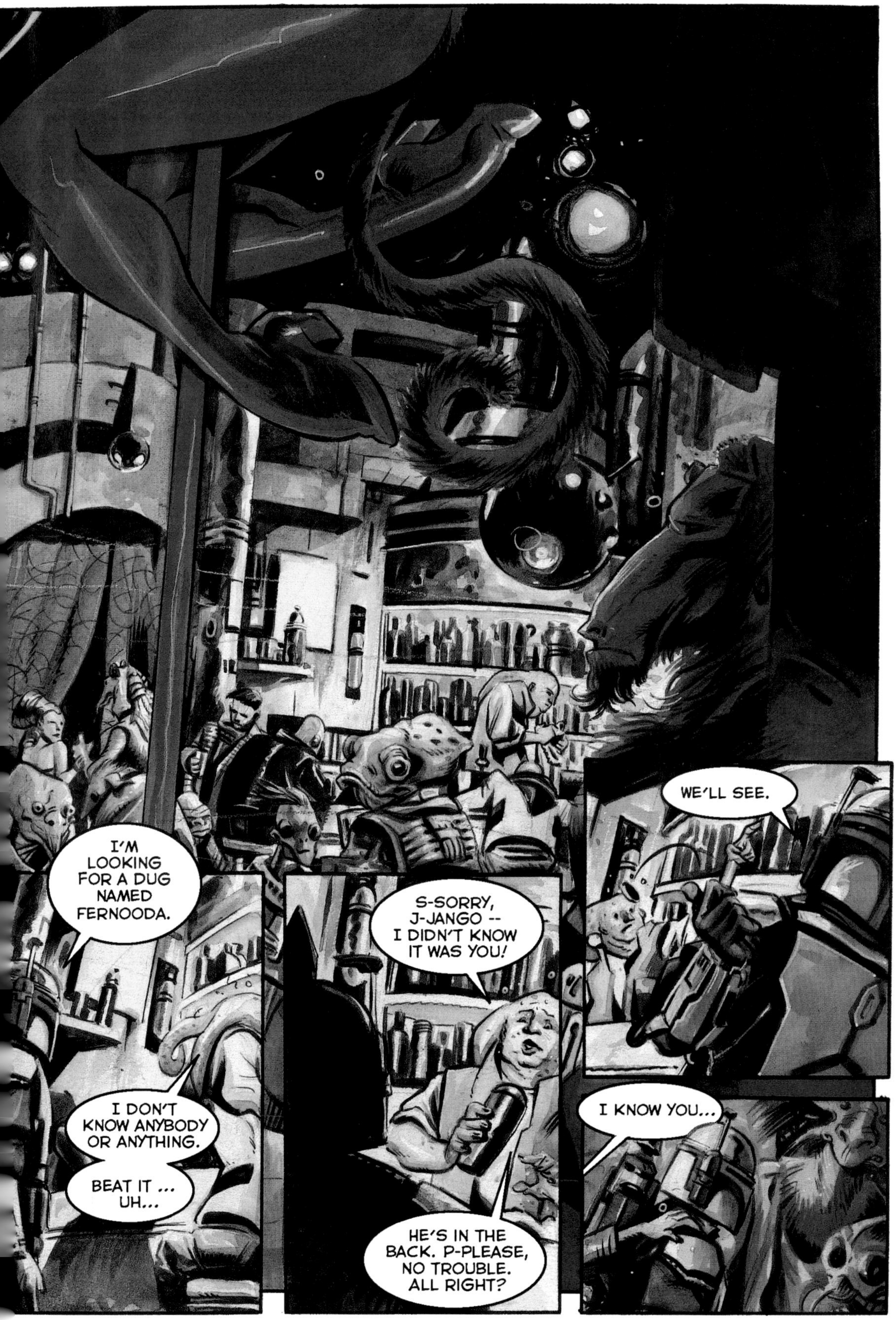
I'M LOOKING FOR A DUG NAMED FERNOODA.
I DON'T KNOW ANYBODY OR ANYTHING.
BEAT IT ... UH...
S-SORRY, J-JANGO -- I DIDN'T KNOW IT WAS YOU!
HE'S IN THE BACK. P-PLEASE, NO TROUBLE. ALL RIGHT?
WE'LL SEE.
I KNOW YOU...

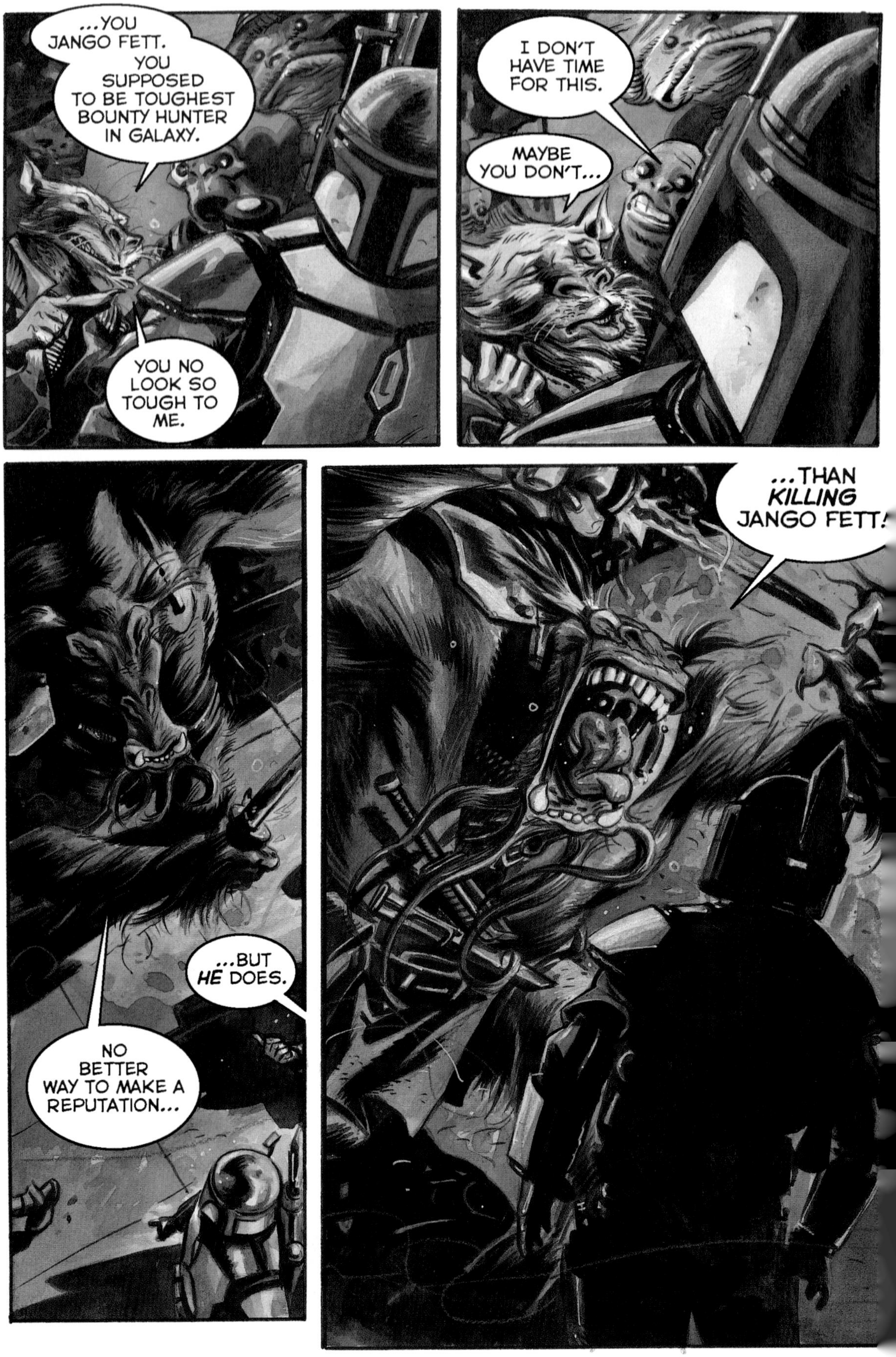
...YOU JANGO FETT.
YOU SUPPOSED TO BE TOUGHEST BOUNTY HUNTER IN GALAXY.
YOU NO LOOK SO TOUGH TO ME.
I DON'T HAVE TIME FOR THIS.
MAYBE YOU DON'T...
...BUT *HE* DOES.
NO BETTER WAY TO MAKE A REPUTATION...
...THAN *KILLING* JANGO FETT!

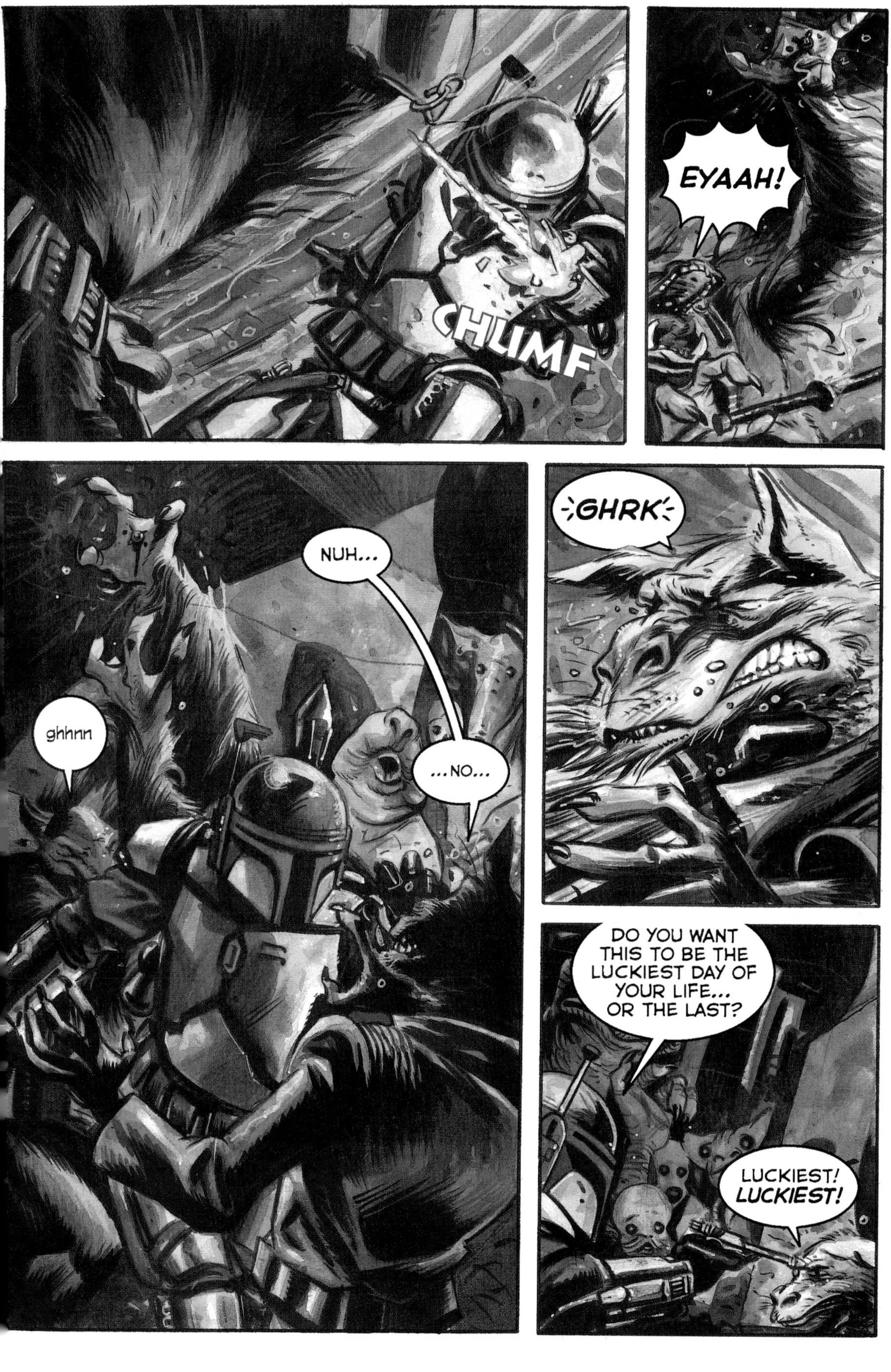
CHUMF
EYAAH!
NUH...
...NO...
ghhnn
GHRK
DO YOU WANT THIS TO BE THE LUCKIEST DAY OF YOUR LIFE... OR THE LAST?
LUCKIEST! LUCKIEST!

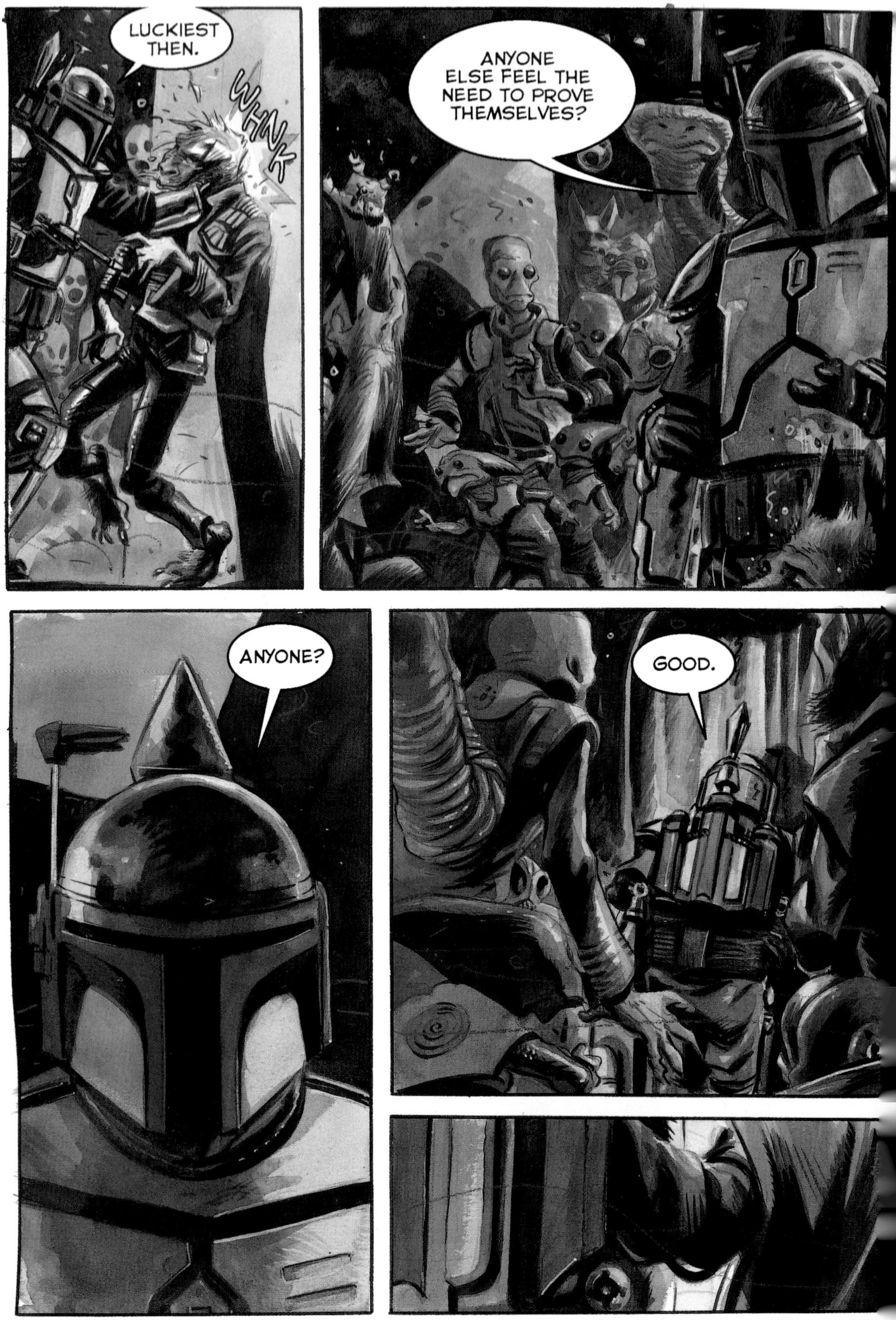
LUCKIEST THEN.
WHNK
ANYONE ELSE FEEL THE NEED TO PROVE THEMSELVES?
ANYONE?
GOOD.

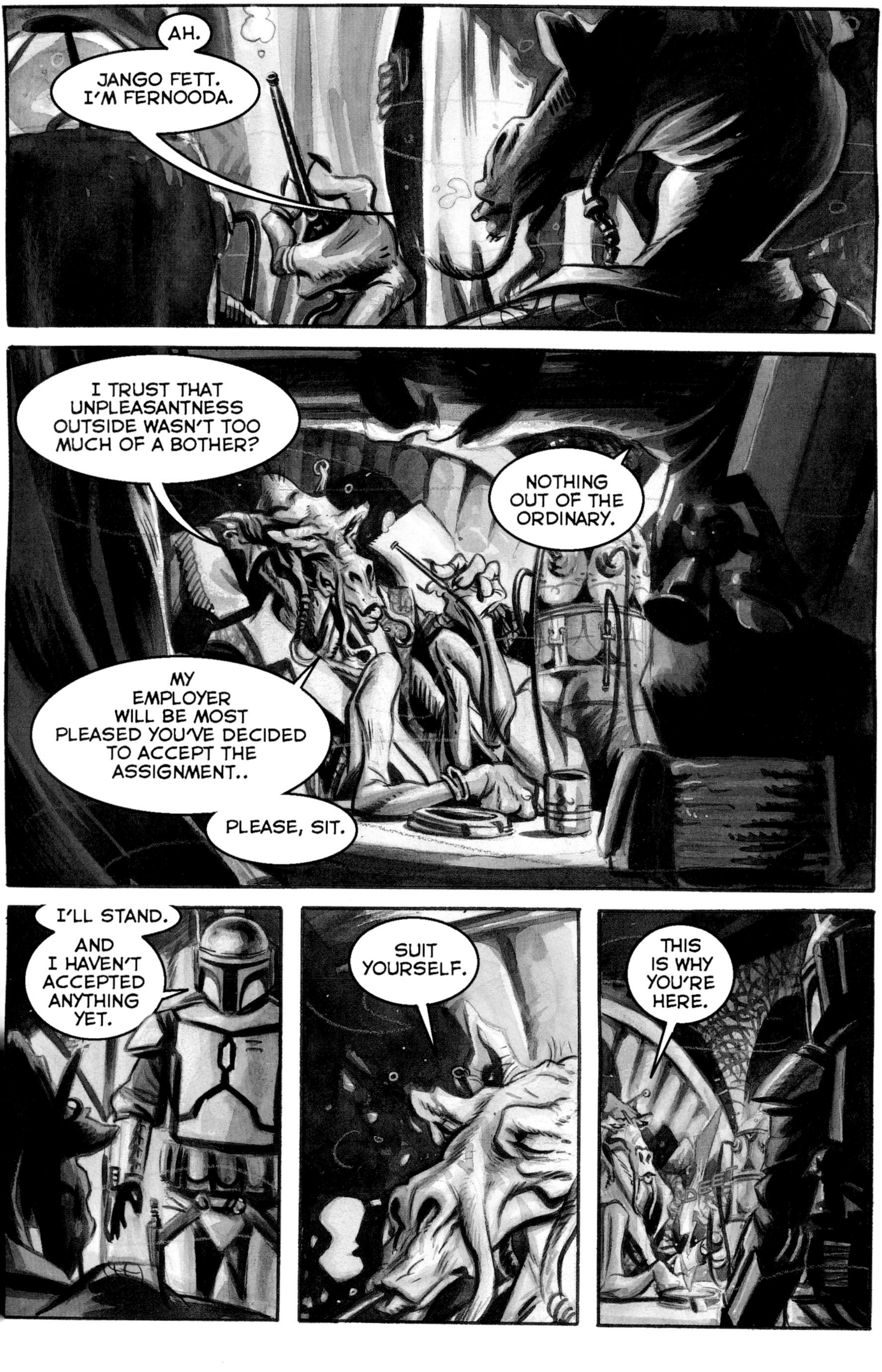
AH.
JANGO FETT. I'M FERNOODA.
I TRUST THAT UNPLEASANTNESS OUTSIDE WASN'T TOO MUCH OF A BOTHER?
NOTHING OUT OF THE ORDINARY.
MY EMPLOYER WILL BE MOST PLEASED YOU'VE DECIDED TO ACCEPT THE ASSIGNMENT..
PLEASE, SIT.
I'LL STAND.
AND I HAVEN'T ACCEPTED ANYTHING YET.
SUIT YOURSELF.
THIS IS WHY YOU'RE HERE.

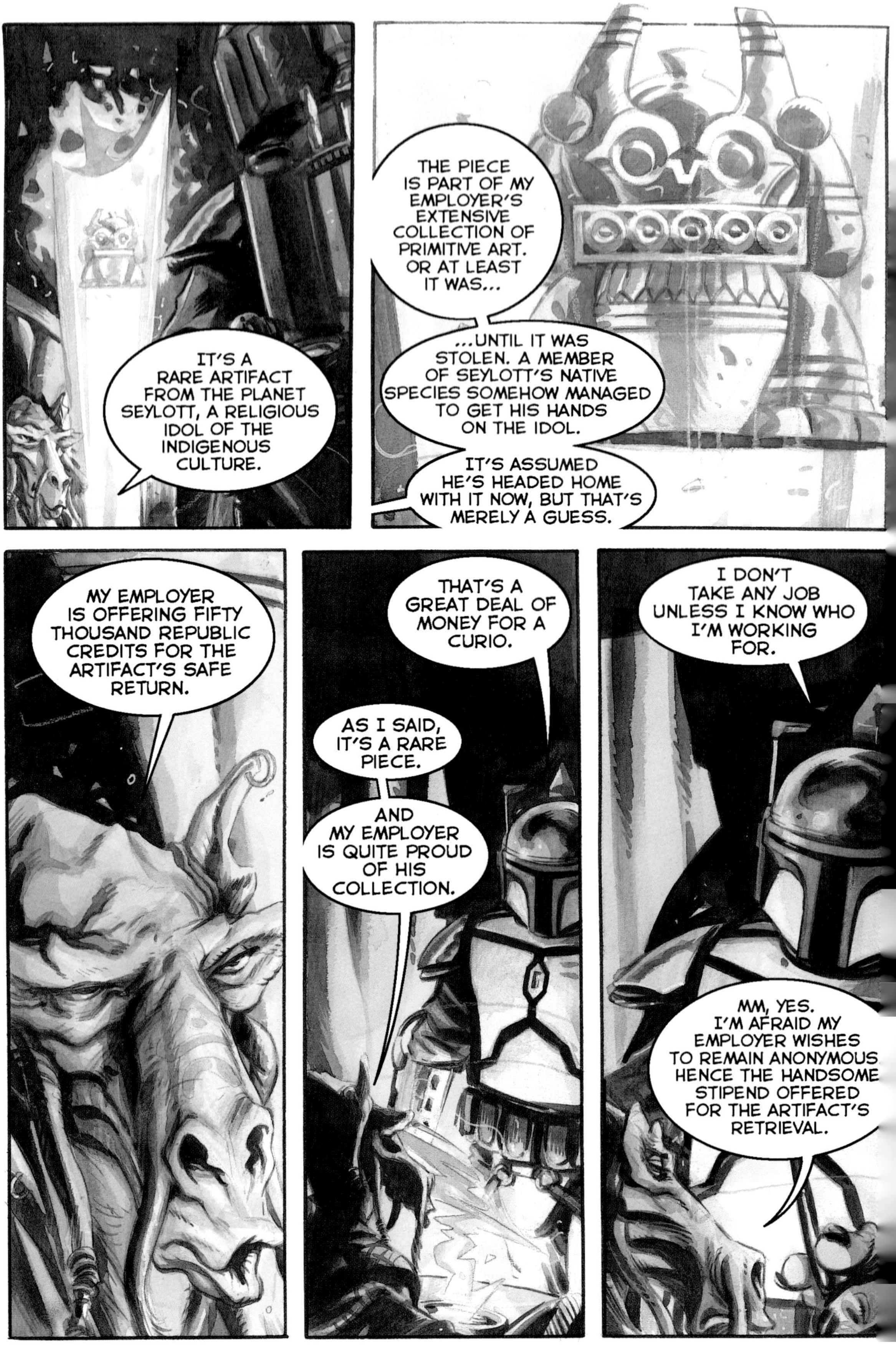
IT'S A RARE ARTIFACT FROM THE PLANET SEYLOTT, A RELIGIOUS IDOL OF THE INDIGENOUS CULTURE.
THE PIECE IS PART OF MY EMPLOYER'S EXTENSIVE COLLECTION OF PRIMITIVE ART. OR AT LEAST IT WAS...
...UNTIL IT WAS STOLEN. A MEMBER OF SEYLOTT'S NATIVE SPECIES SOMEHOW MANAGED TO GET HIS HANDS ON THE IDOL.
IT'S ASSUMED HE'S HEADED HOME WITH IT NOW, BUT THAT'S MERELY A GUESS.
MY EMPLOYER IS OFFERING FIFTY THOUSAND REPUBLIC CREDITS FOR THE ARTIFACT'S SAFE RETURN.
THAT'S A GREAT DEAL OF MONEY FOR A CURIO.
AS I SAID, IT'S A RARE PIECE.
AND MY EMPLOYER IS QUITE PROUD OF HIS COLLECTION.
I DON'T TAKE ANY JOB UNLESS I KNOW WHO I'M WORKING FOR.
MM, YES. I'M AFRAID MY EMPLOYER WISHES TO REMAIN ANONYMOUS HENCE THE HANDSOME STIPEND OFFERED FOR THE ARTIFACT'S RETRIEVAL.

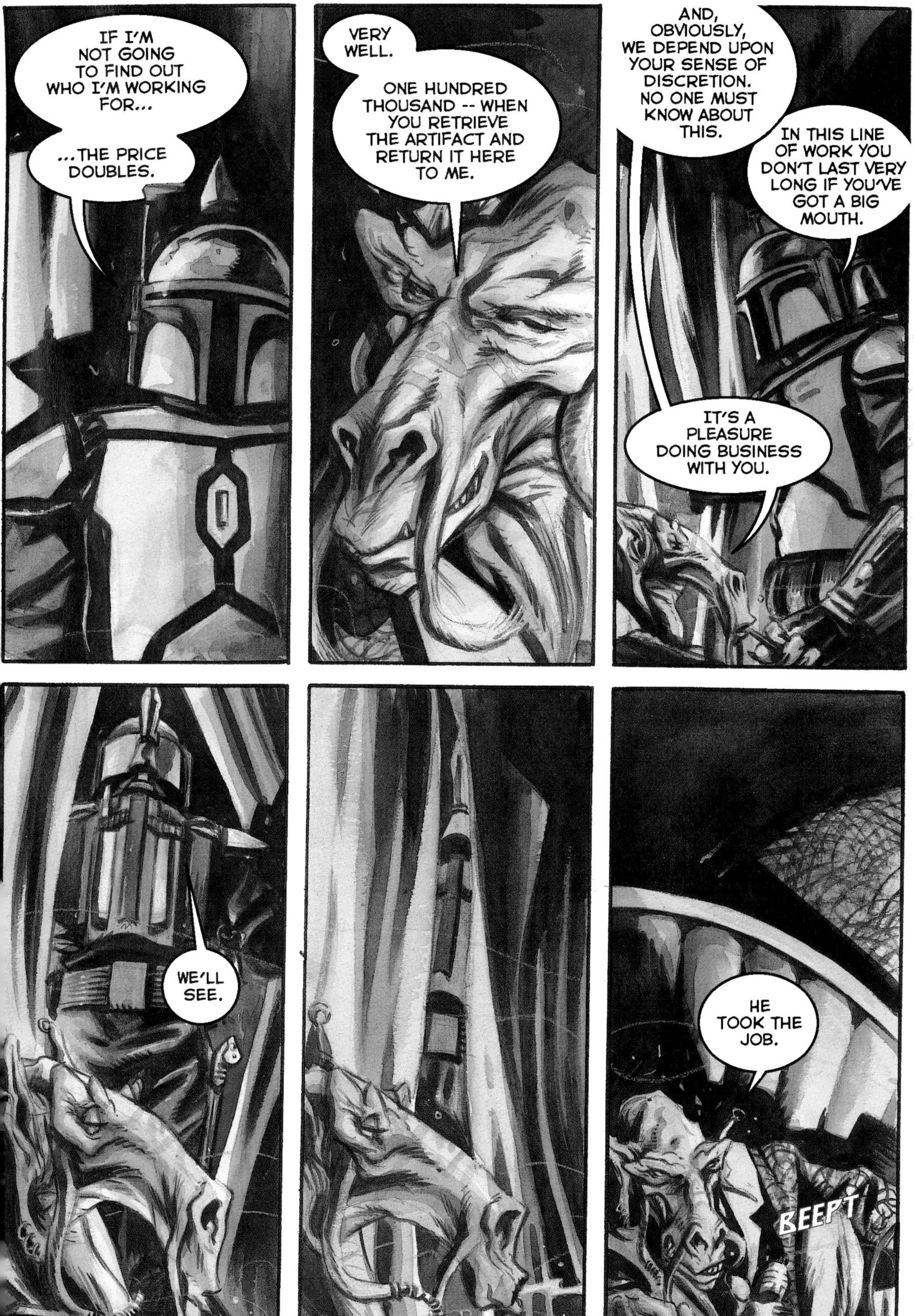
IF I'M NOT GOING TO FIND OUT WHO I'M WORKING FOR...
...THE PRICE DOUBLES.
VERY WELL.
ONE HUNDRED THOUSAND -- WHEN YOU RETRIEVE THE ARTIFACT AND RETURN IT HERE TO ME.
AND, OBVIOUSLY, WE DEPEND UPON YOUR SENSE OF DISCRETION. NO ONE MUST KNOW ABOUT THIS.
IN THIS LINE OF WORK YOU DON'T LAST VERY LONG IF YOU'VE GOT A BIG MOUTH.
IT'S A PLEASURE DOING BUSINESS WITH YOU.
WE'LL SEE.
HE TOOK THE JOB.
BEEPT

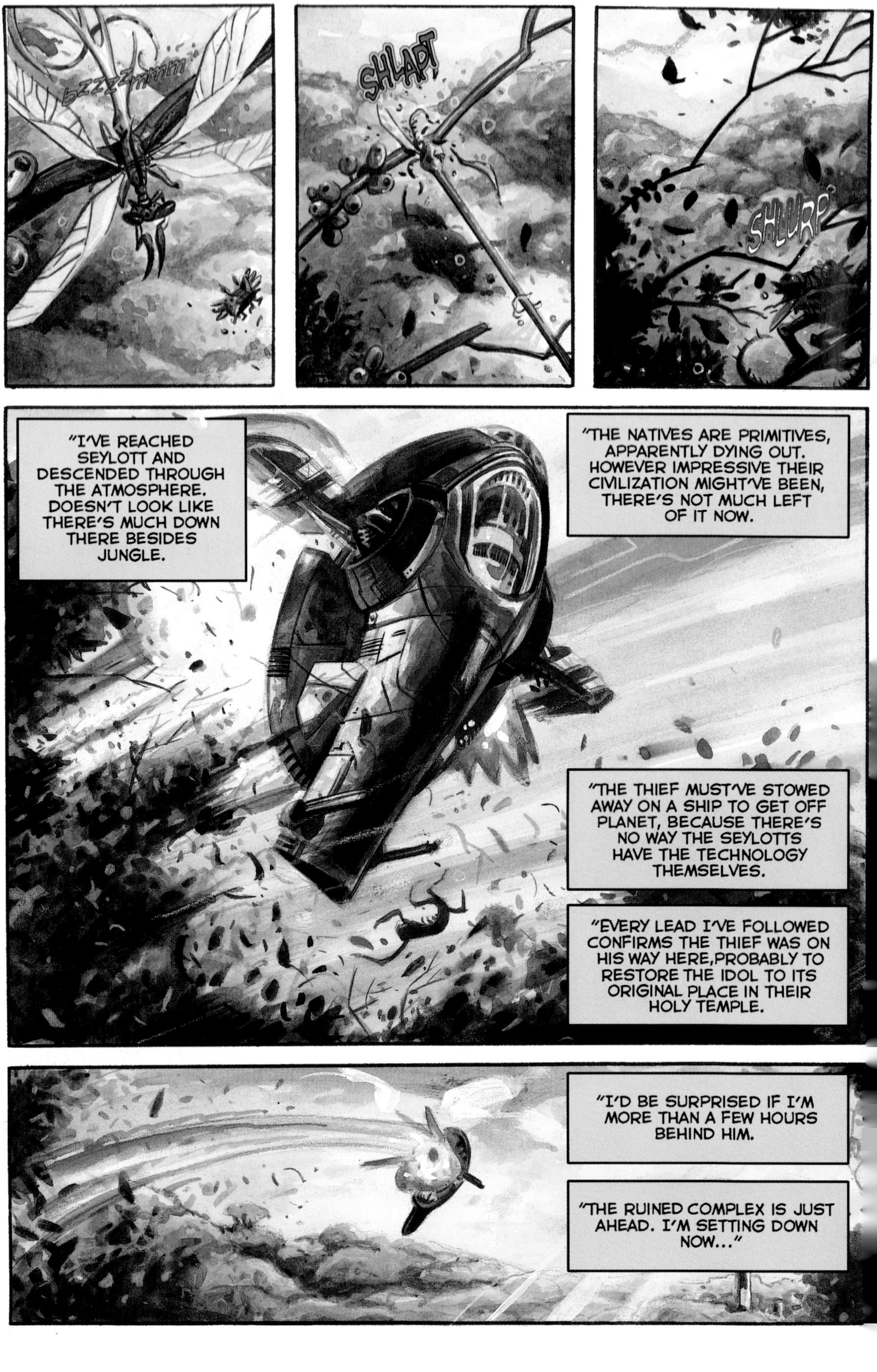
bZZZZmmm
SHLAPT
SHLURP
"I'VE REACHED SEYLOTT AND DESCENDED THROUGH THE ATMOSPHERE. DOESN'T LOOK LIKE THERE'S MUCH DOWN THERE BESIDES JUNGLE.
"THE NATIVES ARE PRIMITIVES, APPARENTLY DYING OUT. HOWEVER IMPRESSIVE THEIR CIVILIZATION MIGHT'VE BEEN, THERE'S NOT MUCH LEFT OF IT NOW.
"THE THIEF MUST'VE STOWED AWAY ON A SHIP TO GET OFF PLANET, BECAUSE THERE'S NO WAY THE SEYLOTTS HAVE THE TECHNOLOGY THEMSELVES.
"EVERY LEAD I'VE FOLLOWED CONFIRMS THE THIEF WAS ON HIS WAY HERE,PROBABLY TO RESTORE THE IDOL TO ITS ORIGINAL PLACE IN THEIR HOLY TEMPLE.
"I'D BE SURPRISED IF I'M MORE THAN A FEW HOURS BEHIND HIM.
"THE RUINED COMPLEX IS JUST AHEAD. I'M SETTING DOWN NOW..."

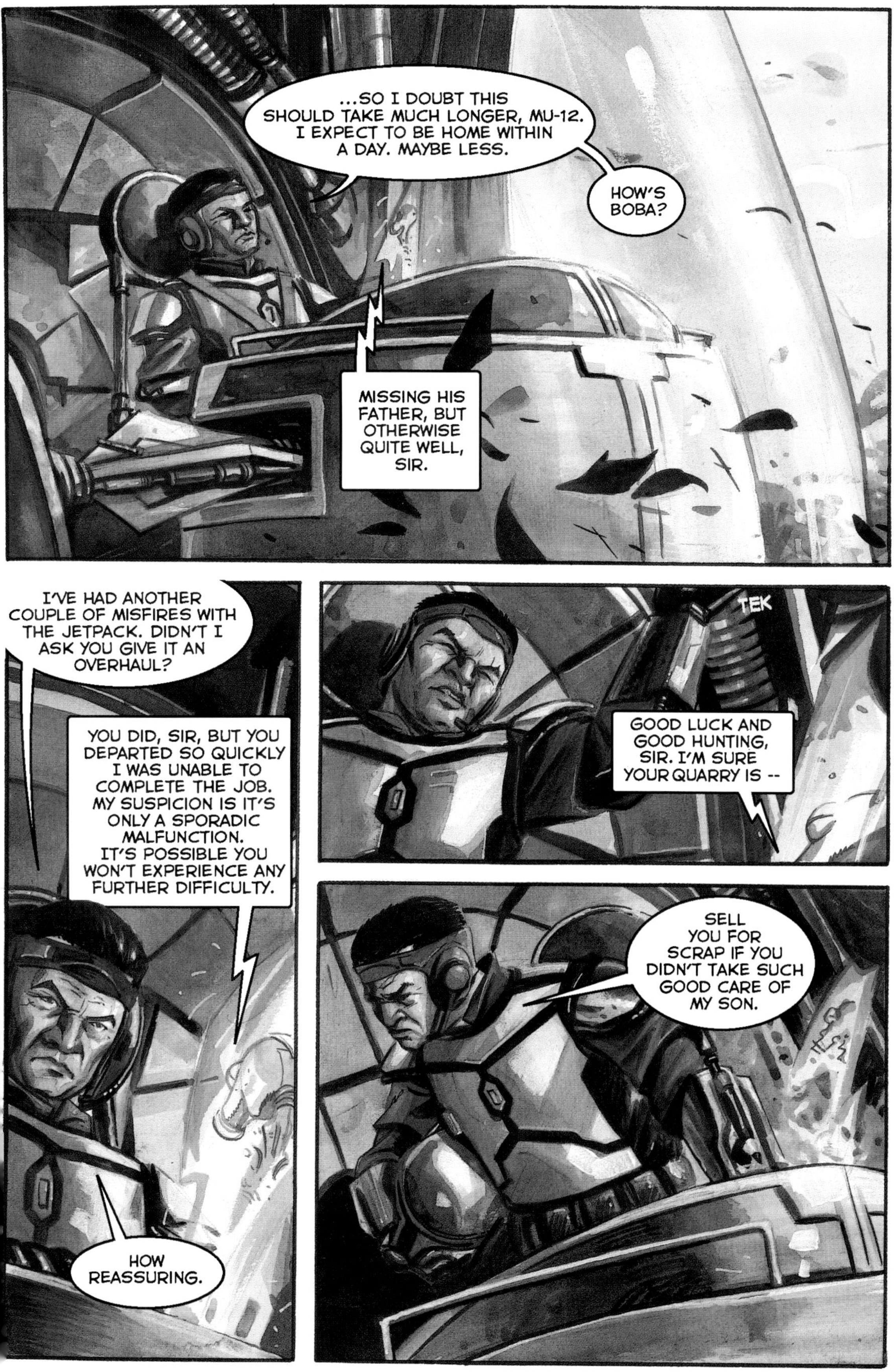
...SO I DOUBT THIS SHOULD TAKE MUCH LONGER, MU-12. I EXPECT TO BE HOME WITHIN A DAY. MAYBE LESS.
HOW'S BOBA?
MISSING HIS FATHER, BUT OTHERWISE QUITE WELL, SIR.
I'VE HAD ANOTHER COUPLE OF MISFIRES WITH THE JETPACK. DIDN'T I ASK YOU GIVE IT AN OVERHAUL?
YOU DID, SIR, BUT YOU DEPARTED SO QUICKLY I WAS UNABLE TO COMPLETE THE JOB. MY SUSPICION IS IT'S ONLY A SPORADIC MALFUNCTION. IT'S POSSIBLE YOU WON'T EXPERIENCE ANY FURTHER DIFFICULTY.
HOW REASSURING.
TEK
GOOD LUCK AND GOOD HUNTING, SIR. I'M SURE YOUR QUARRY IS --
SELL YOU FOR SCRAP IF YOU DIDN'T TAKE SUCH GOOD CARE OF MY SON.

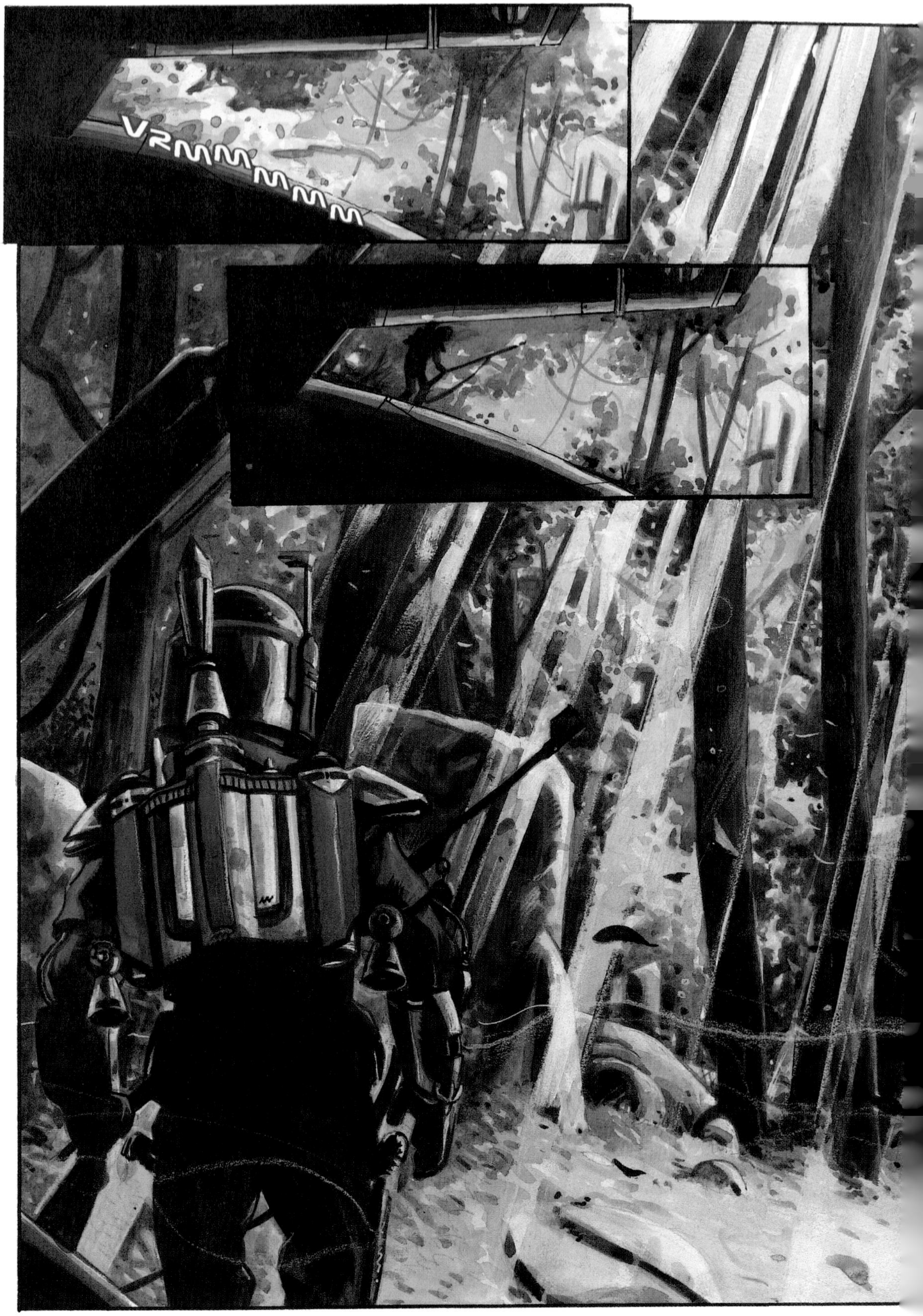
VRMMMMMMM

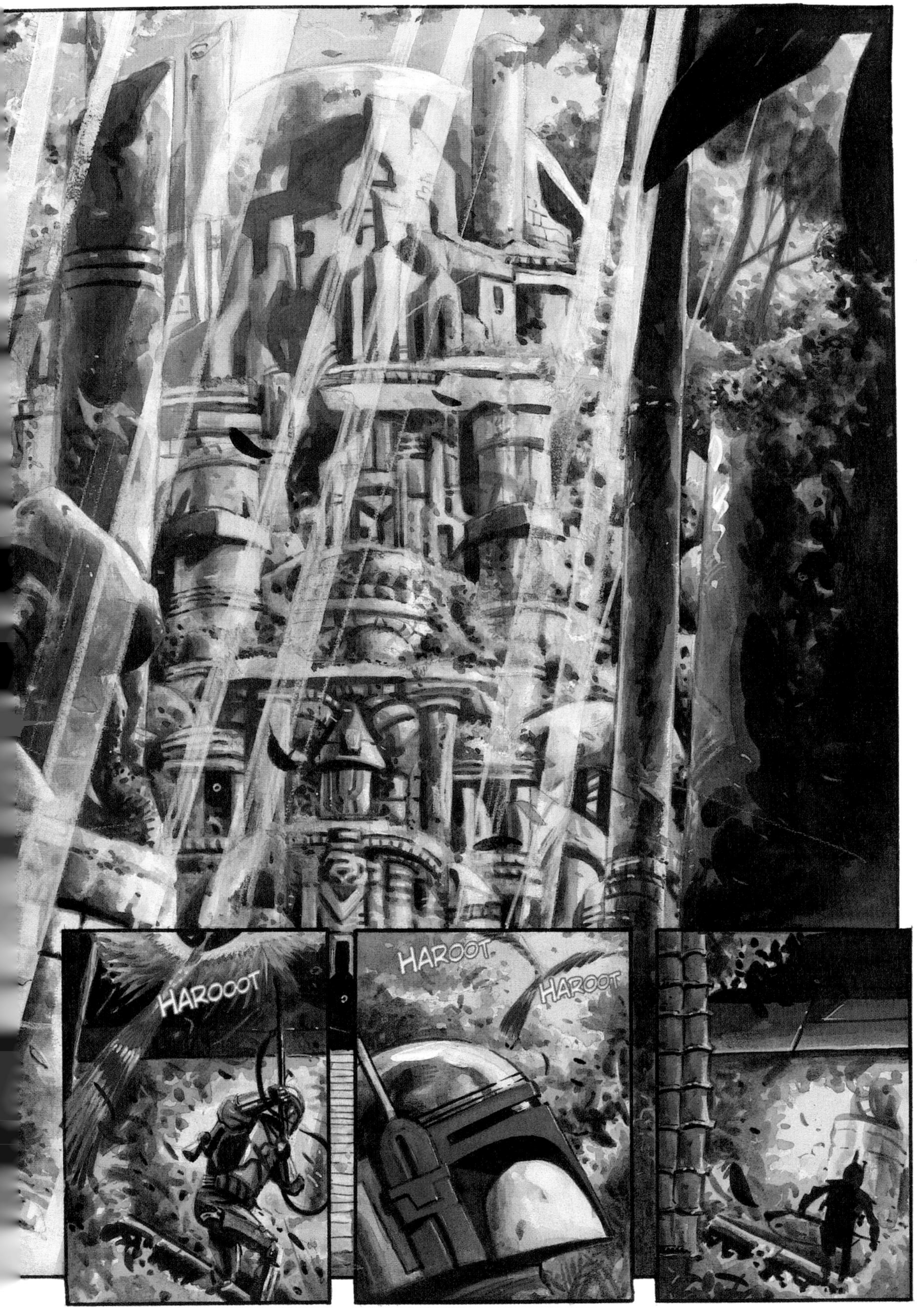
HAROOOT
HAROOT
HAROOT

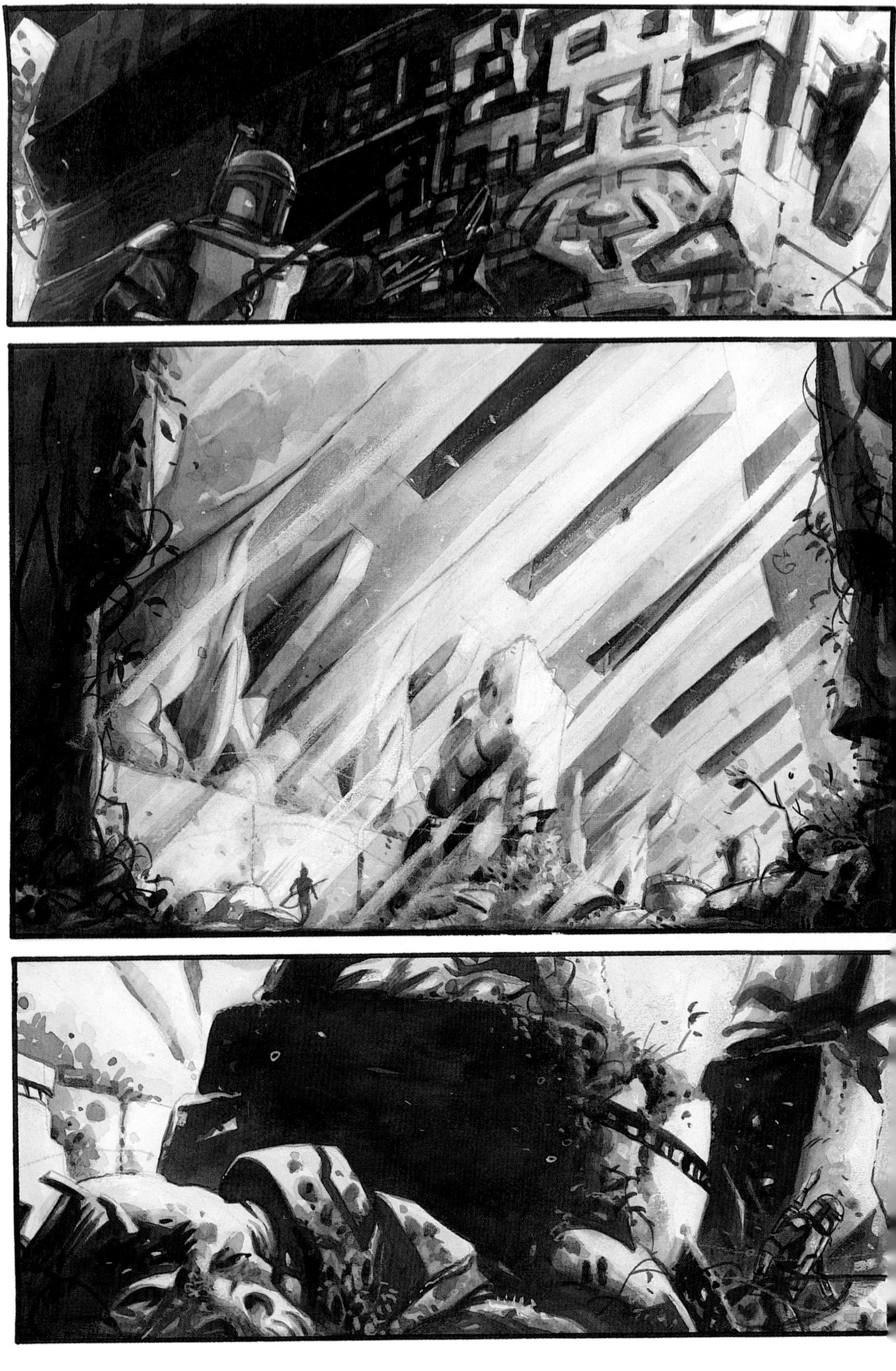

SKrrch

KRRRMBL

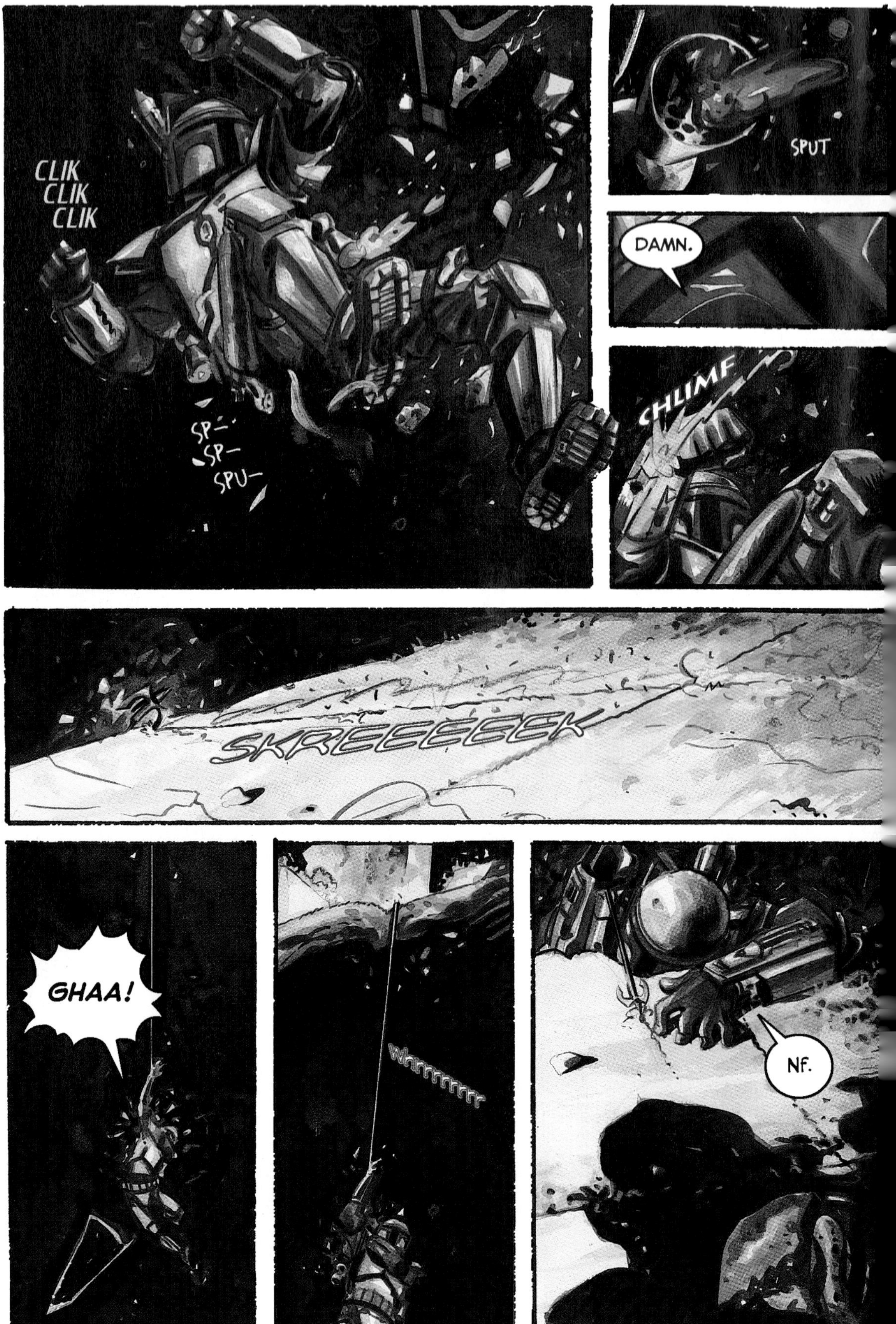
CLIK
CLIK
CLIK
SP—
SP—
SPU—
SPUT
DAMN.
CHLIMF
SKREEEEEEK
GHAA!
Nf.

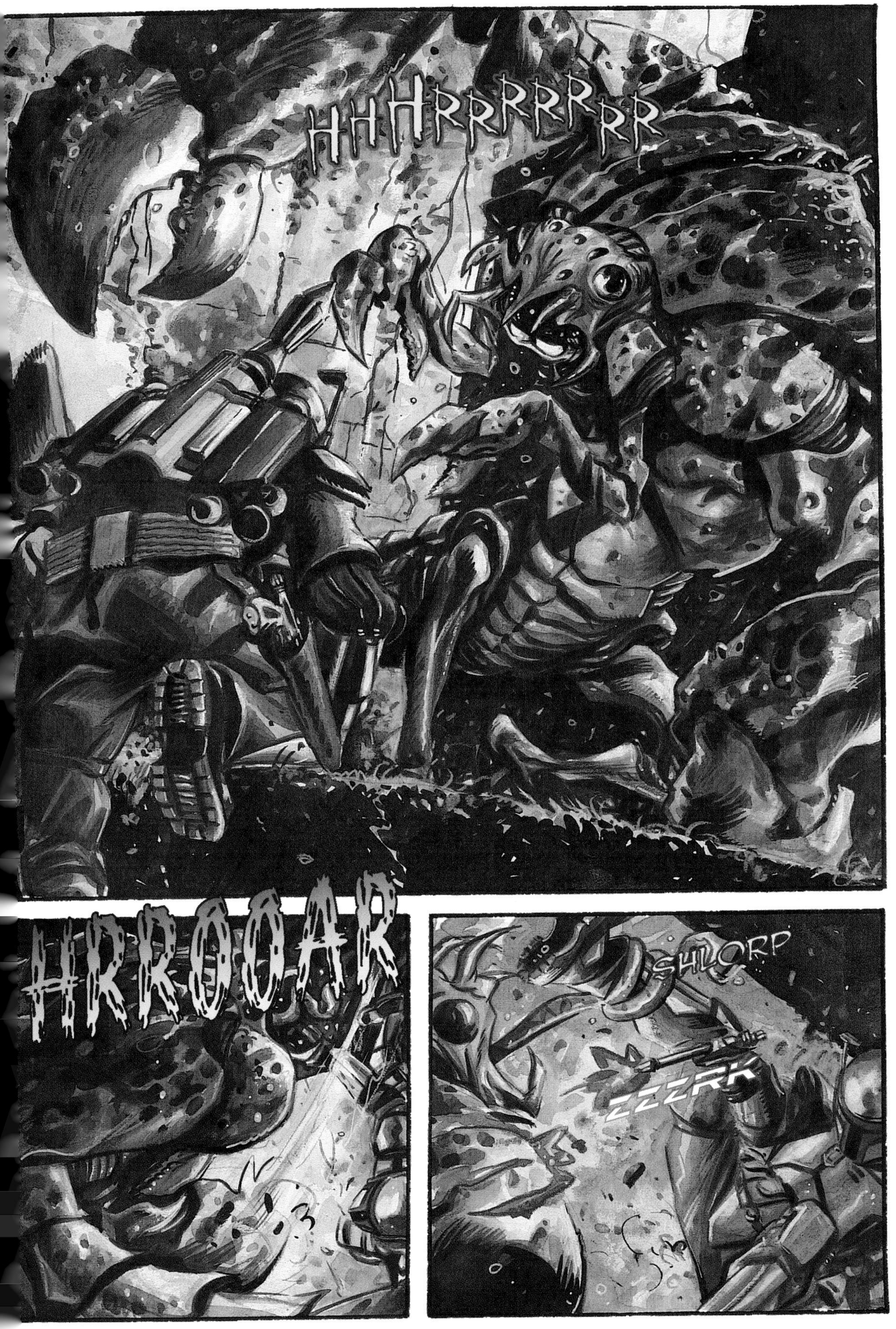
HHHRRRRRR
HRROOAR
SHLORP
ZZZRK

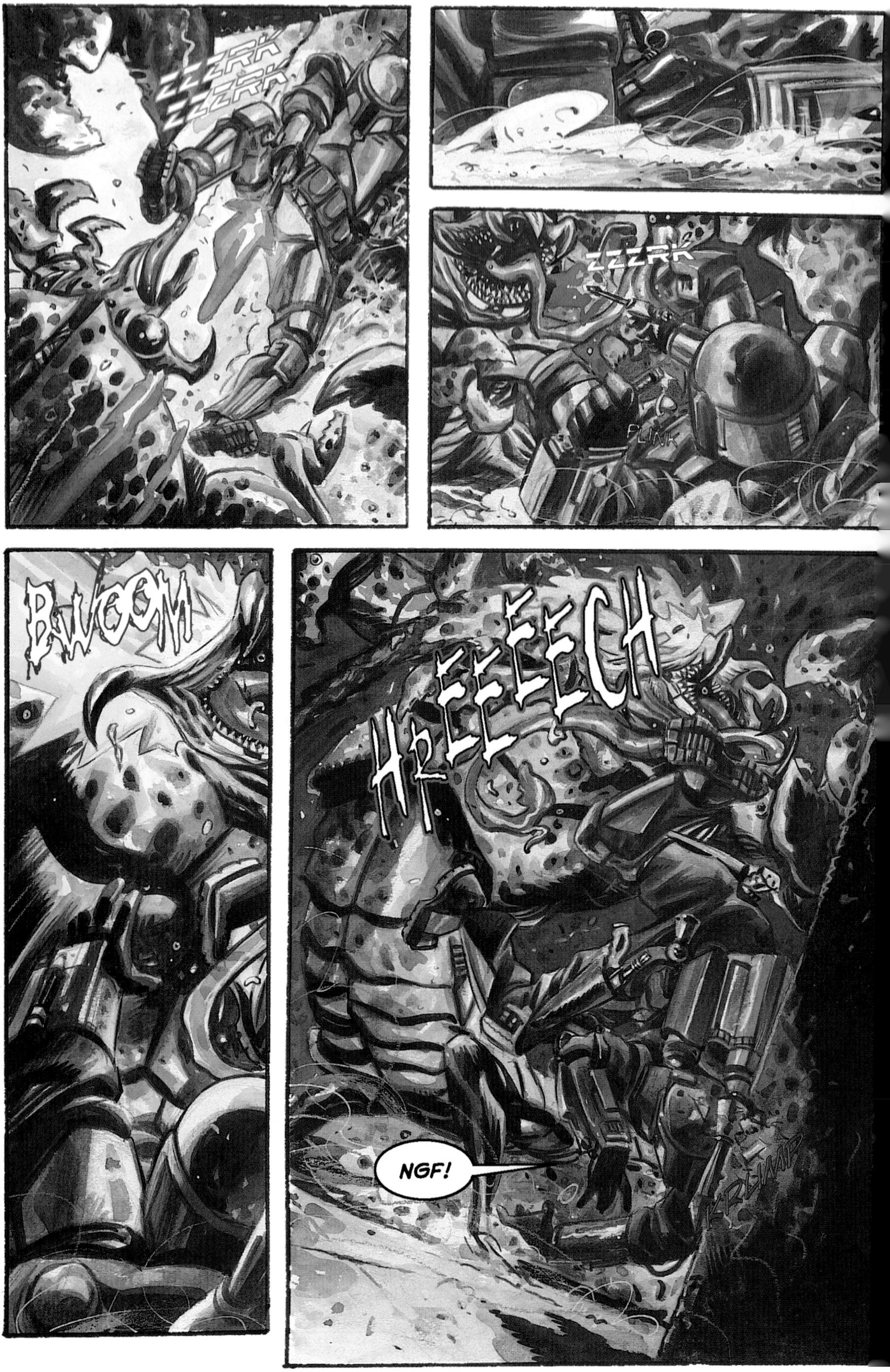
ZZZRK
ZZZRK
ZZZRK
PLINK
BWOOM
HREEEECH
NGF!
KRUMP

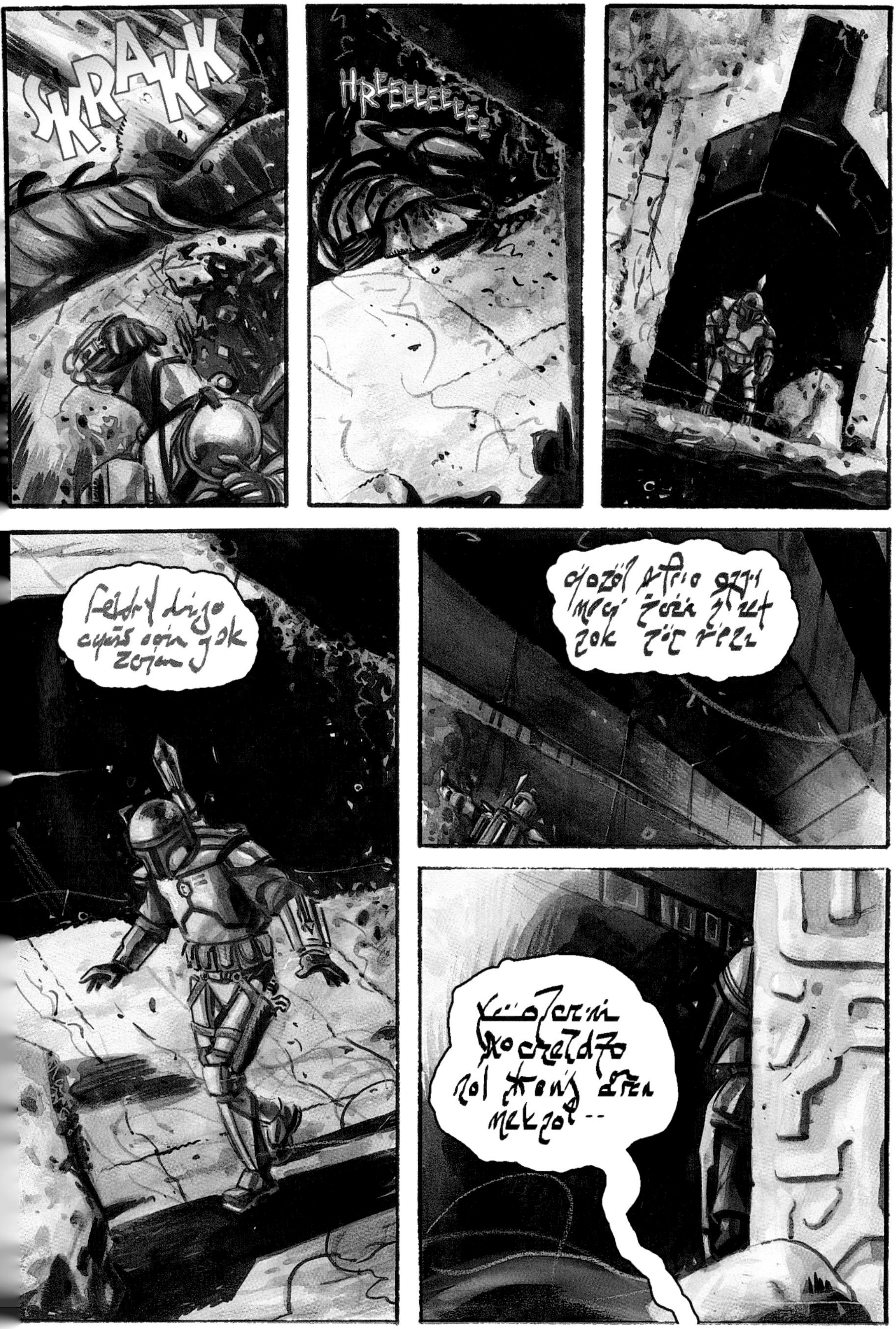
SKRAKK
HREEEEEEEE

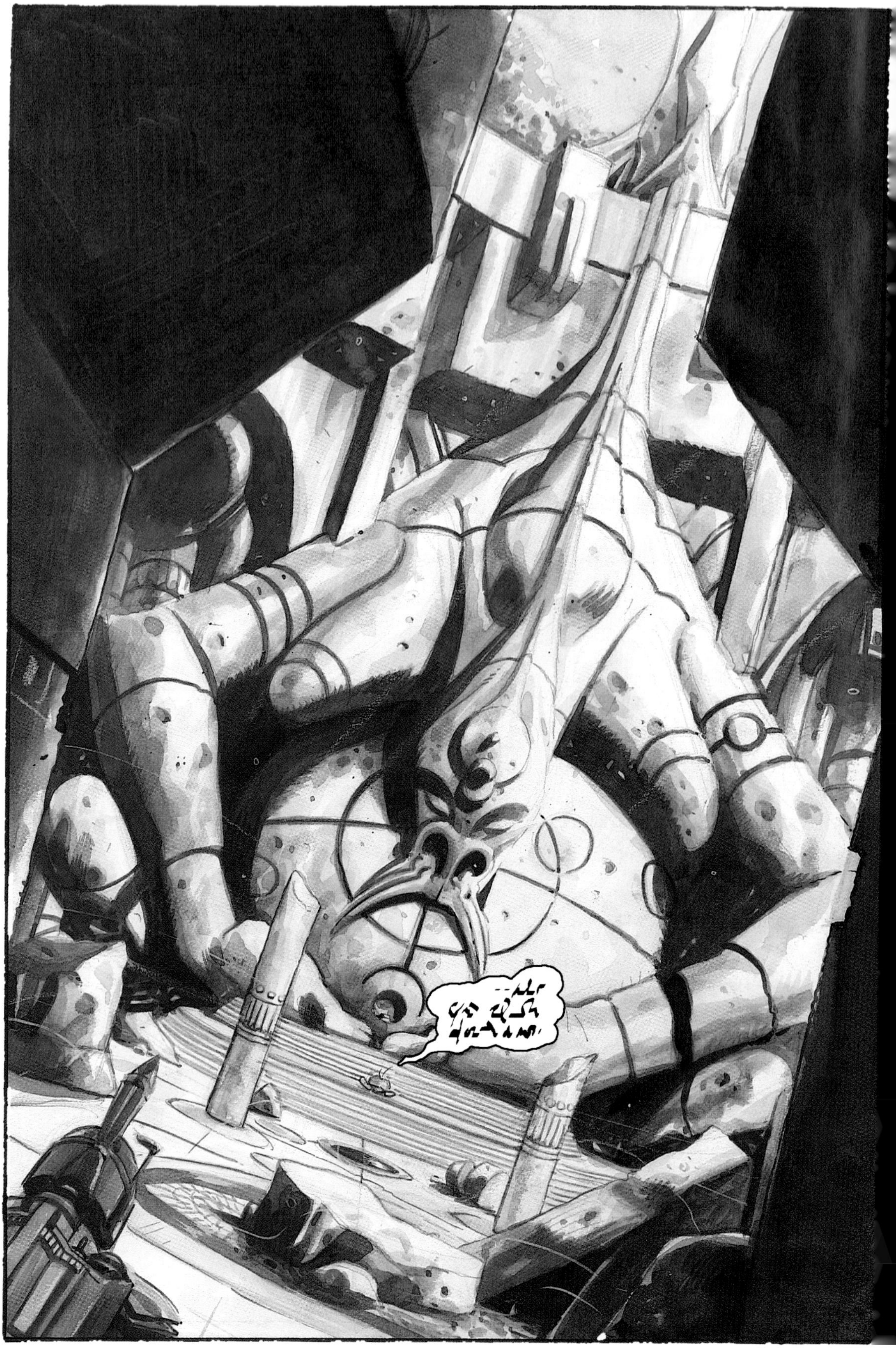

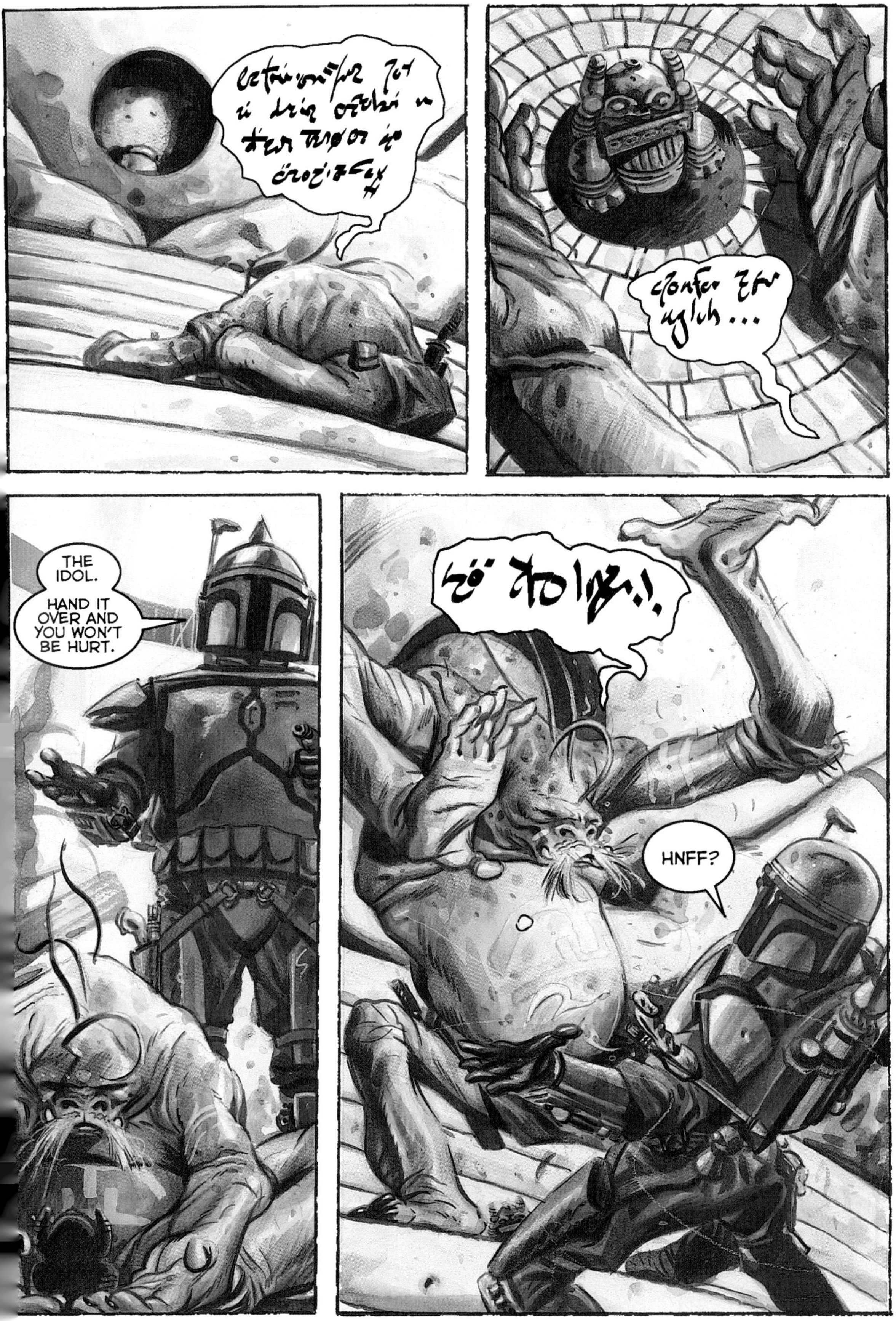
THE IDOL.
HAND IT OVER AND YOU WON'T BE HURT.
HNFF?

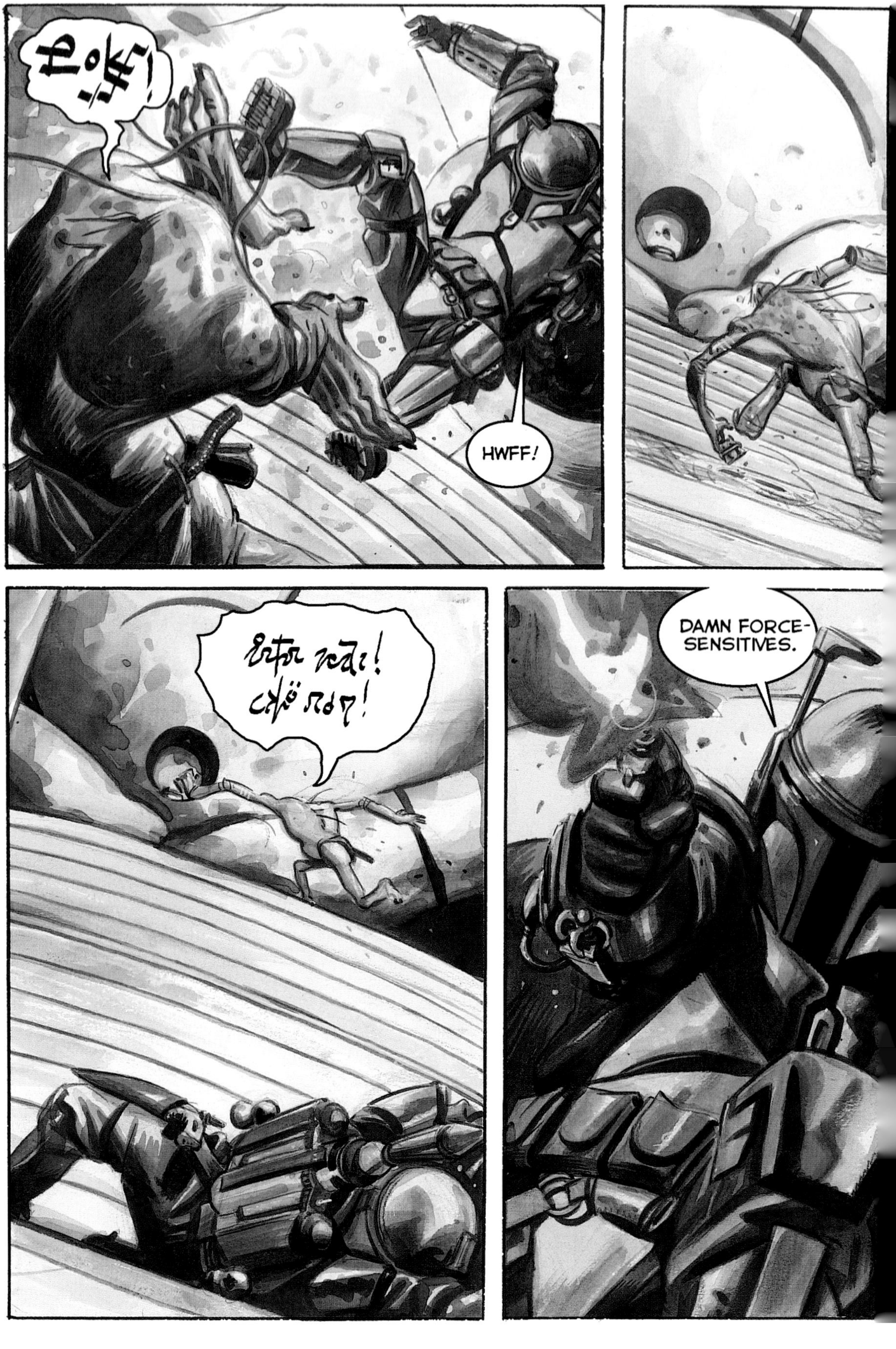
HWFF!
DAMN FORCE-SENSITIVES.

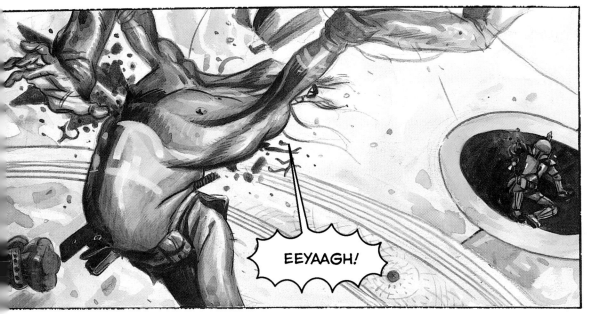

EEYAAGH!

GLLRG...

TINK

...hnngh...

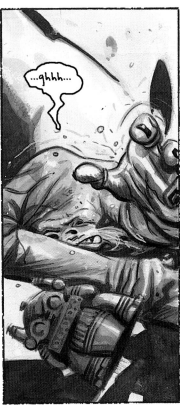

...ghhh...

THIS...

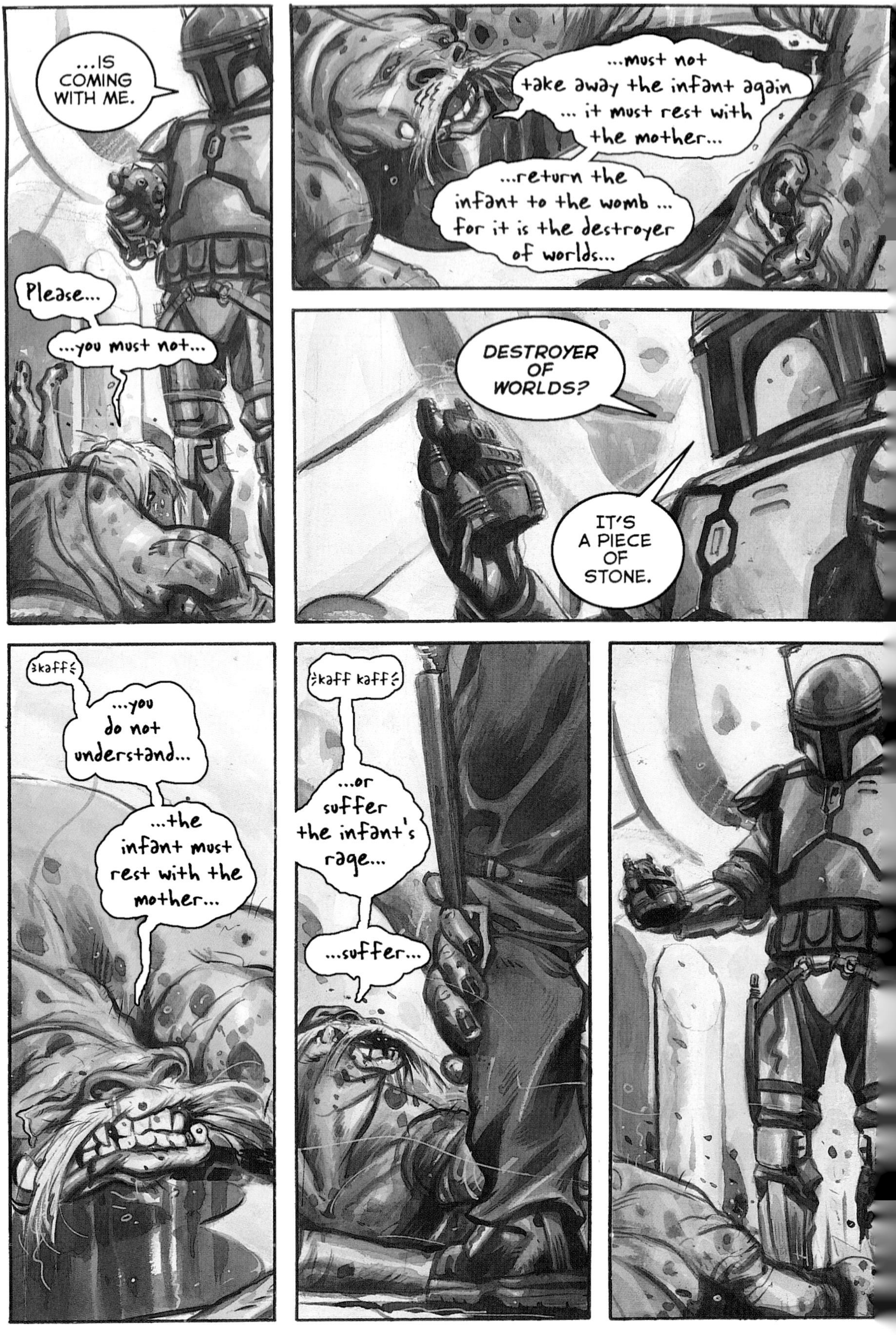
...IS COMING WITH ME.
Please...
...you must not...
...must not take away the infant again ... it must rest with the mother...
...return the infant to the womb ... for it is the destroyer of worlds...
DESTROYER OF WORLDS?
IT'S A PIECE OF STONE.
kaff
...you do not understand...
...the infant must rest with the mother...
kaff kaff
...or suffer the infant's rage...
...suffer...

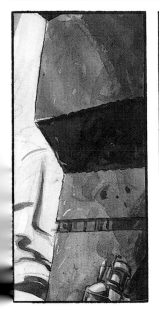

TURN AROUND, JANGO...

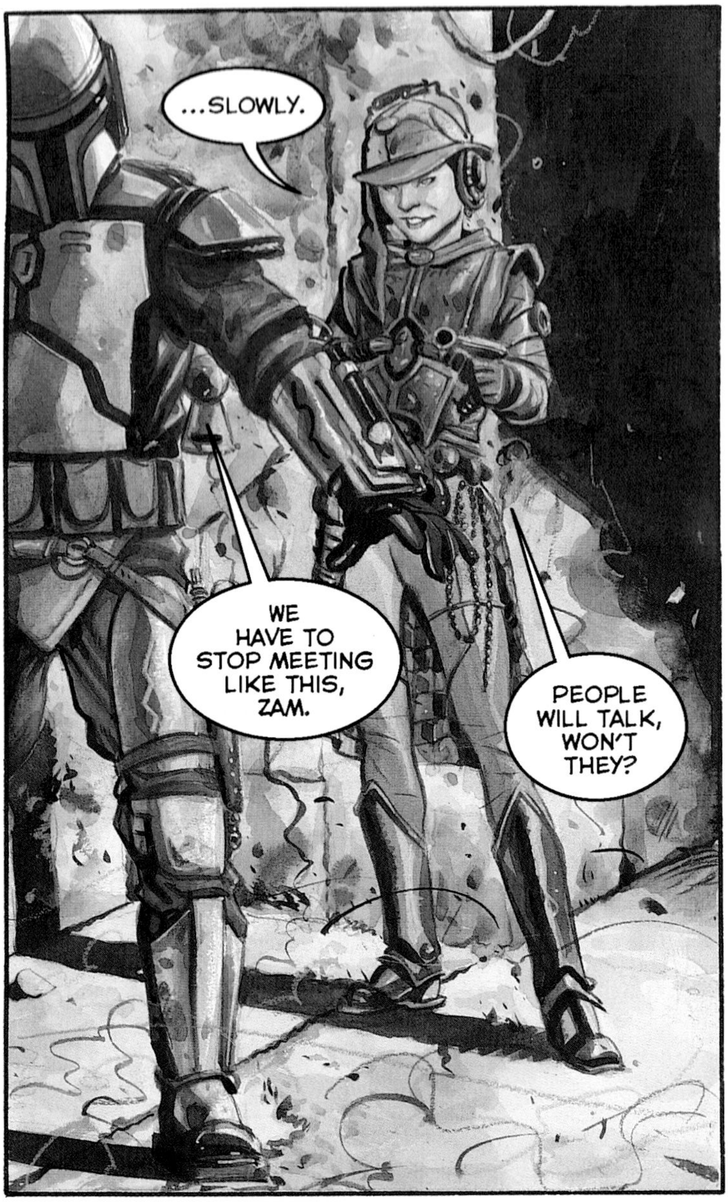
...SLOWLY.
WE HAVE TO STOP MEETING LIKE THIS, ZAM.
PEOPLE WILL TALK, WON'T THEY?

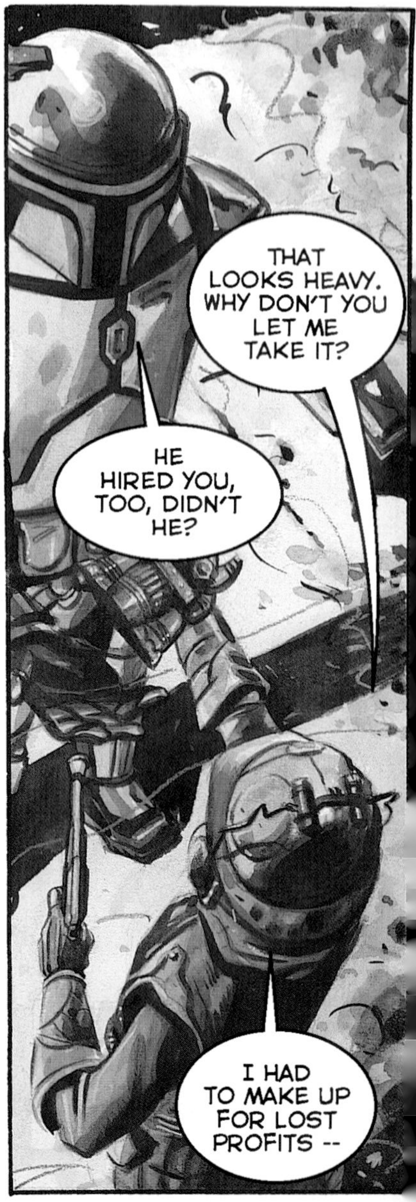
THAT LOOKS HEAVY. WHY DON'T YOU LET ME TAKE IT?
HE HIRED YOU, TOO, DIDN'T HE?
I HAD TO MAKE UP FOR LOST PROFITS --

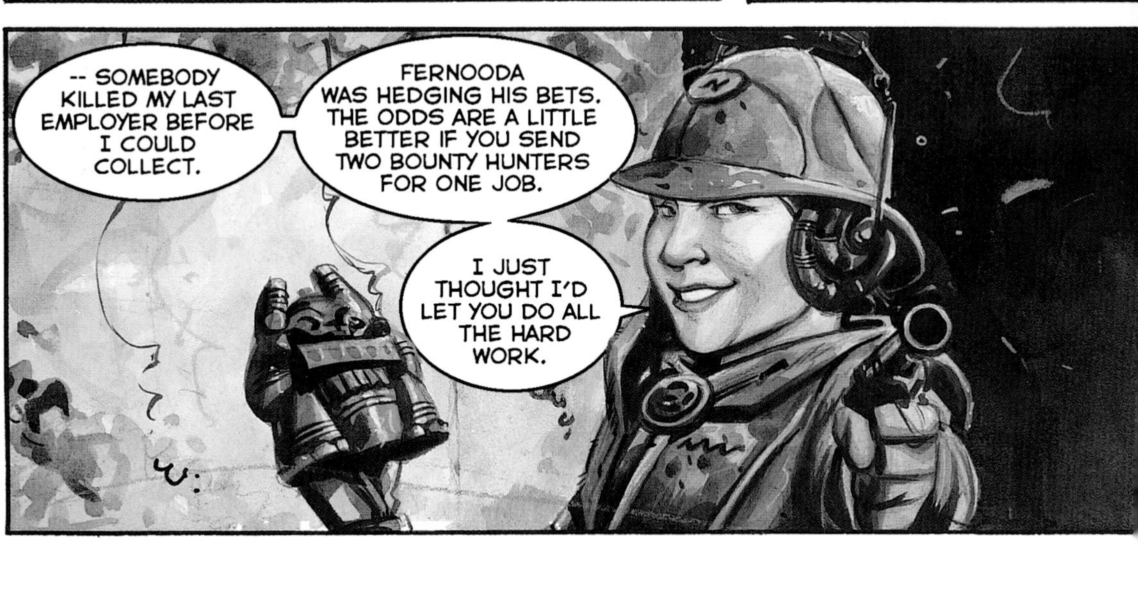
-- SOMEBODY KILLED MY LAST EMPLOYER BEFORE I COULD COLLECT.
FERNOODA WAS HEDGING HIS BETS. THE ODDS ARE A LITTLE BETTER IF YOU SEND TWO BOUNTY HUNTERS FOR ONE JOB.
I JUST THOUGHT I'D LET YOU DO ALL THE HARD WORK.

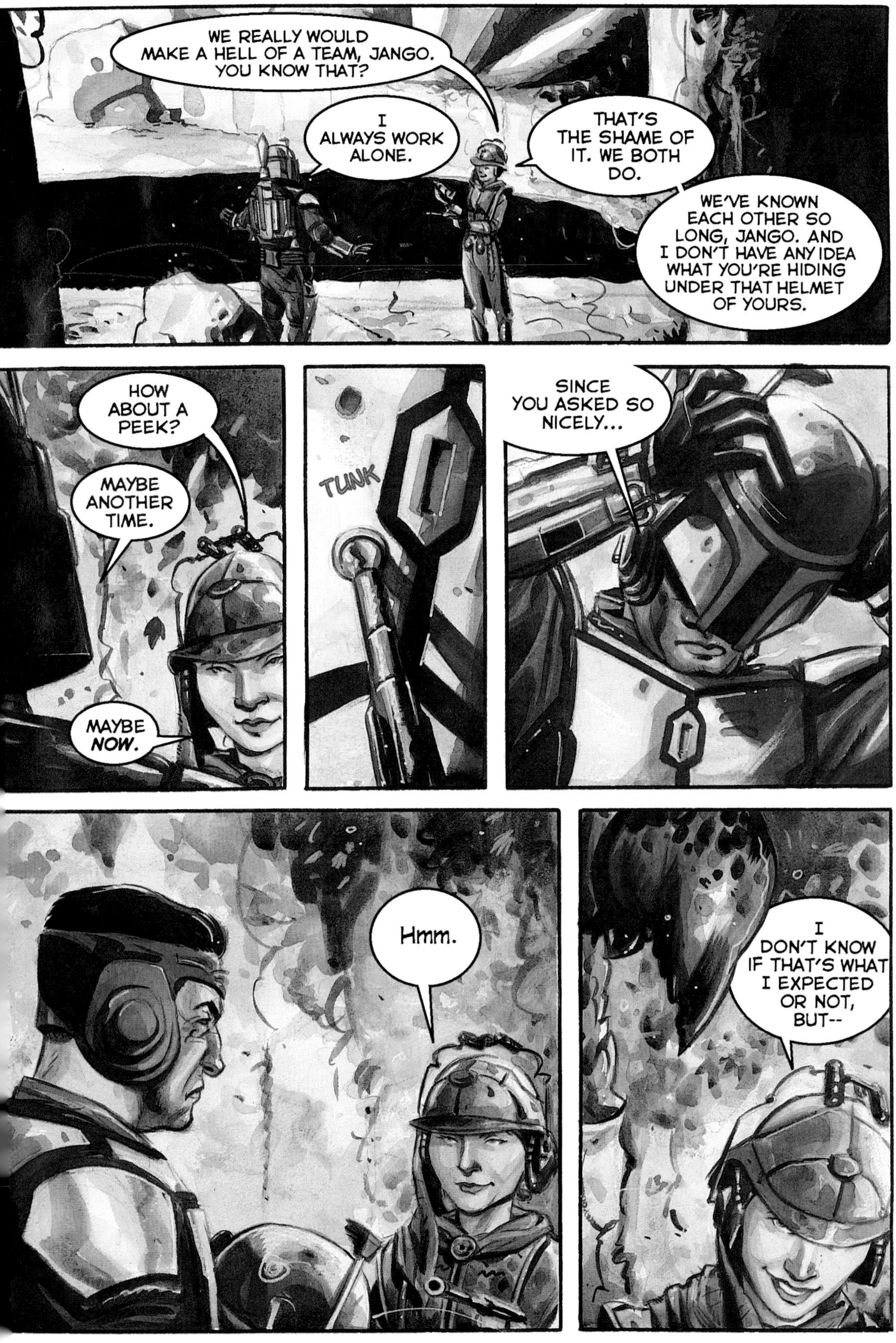
WE REALLY WOULD MAKE A HELL OF A TEAM, JANGO. YOU KNOW THAT?
I ALWAYS WORK ALONE.
THAT'S THE SHAME OF IT. WE BOTH DO.
WE'VE KNOWN EACH OTHER SO LONG, JANGO. AND I DON'T HAVE ANY IDEA WHAT YOU'RE HIDING UNDER THAT HELMET OF YOURS.
HOW ABOUT A PEEK?
MAYBE ANOTHER TIME.
MAYBE *NOW*.
TUNK
SINCE YOU ASKED SO NICELY...
Hmm.
I DON'T KNOW IF THAT'S WHAT I EXPECTED OR NOT, BUT--

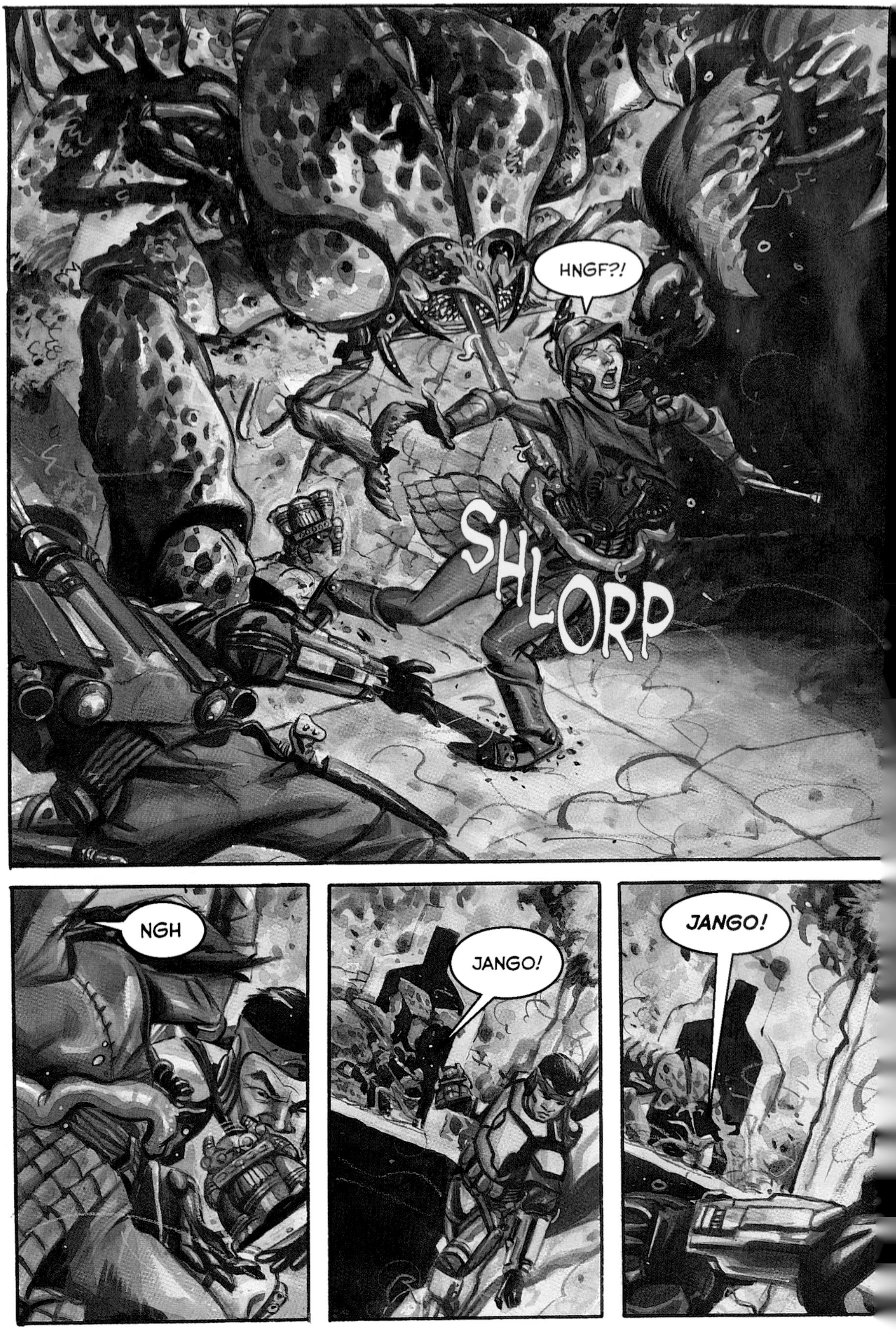
HNGF?!
SHLORP
NGH
JANGO!
JANGO!

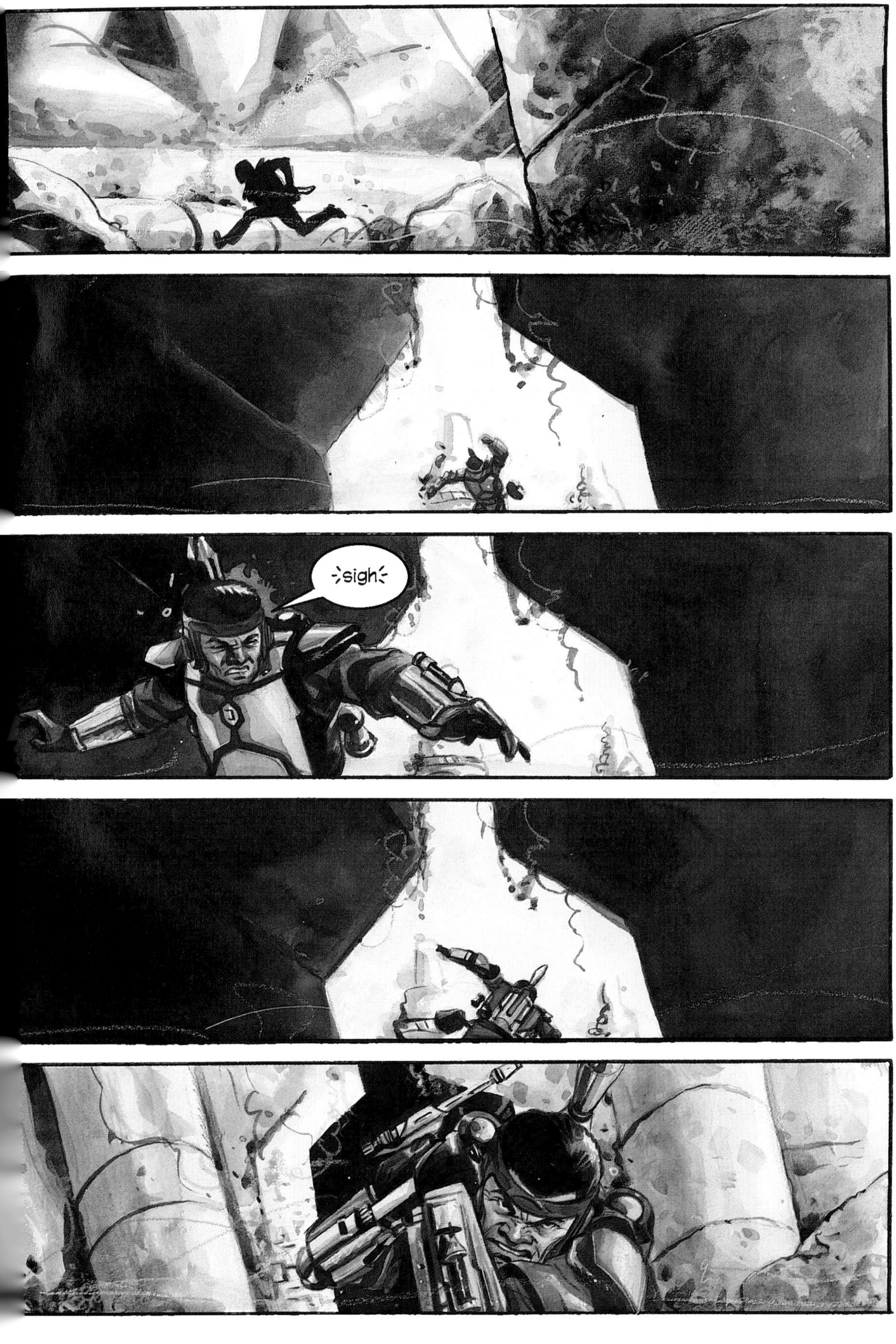
sigh

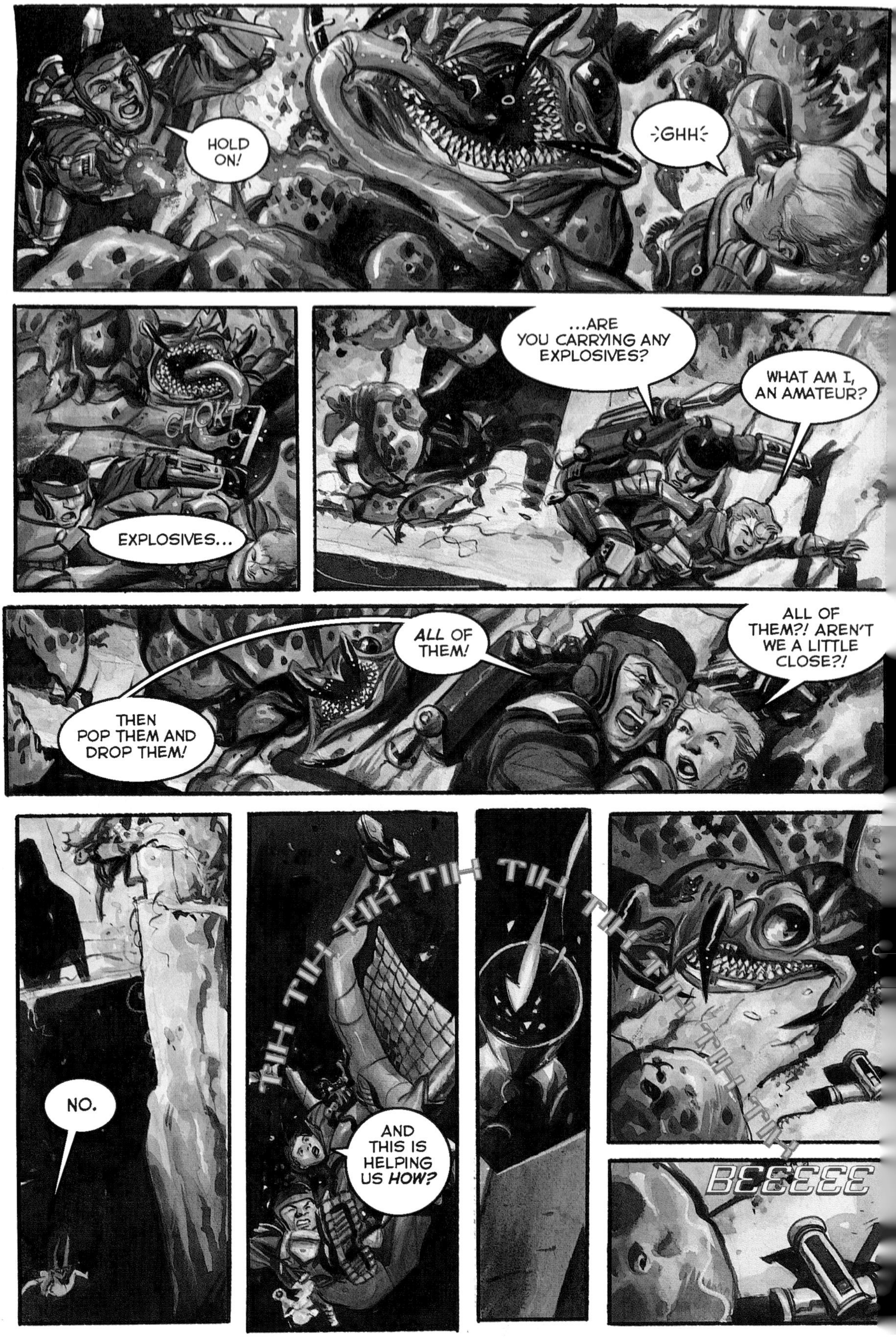

HOLD ON!
-GHH-
CHOKT
EXPLOSIVES...
...ARE YOU CARRYING ANY EXPLOSIVES?
WHAT AM I, AN AMATEUR?
ALL OF THEM!
ALL OF THEM?! AREN'T WE A LITTLE CLOSE?!
THEN POP THEM AND DROP THEM!
NO.
TIH TIH TIH TIH TIH TIH TIH
AND THIS IS HELPING US HOW?
BEEEEE

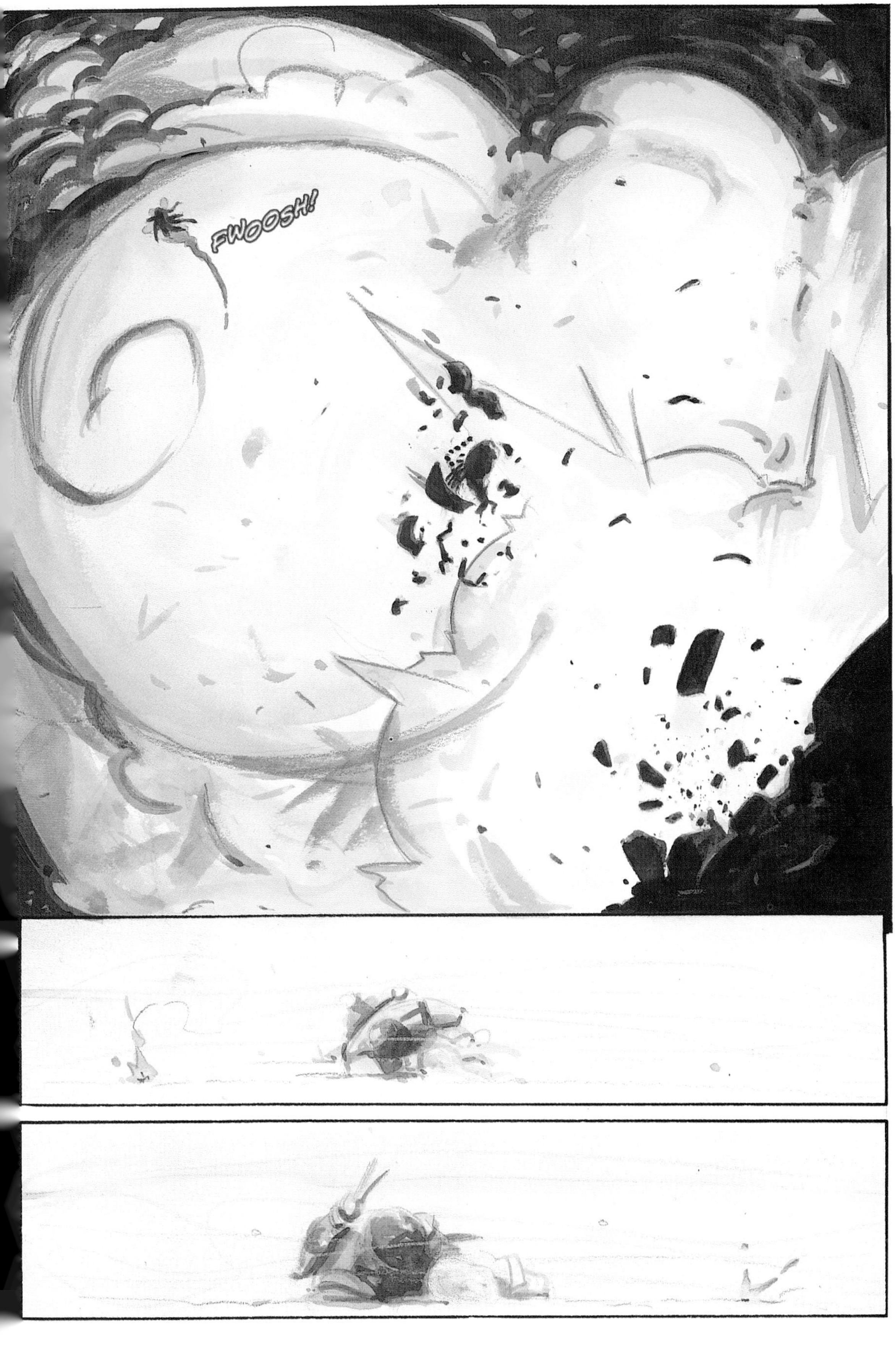
FWOOSH!

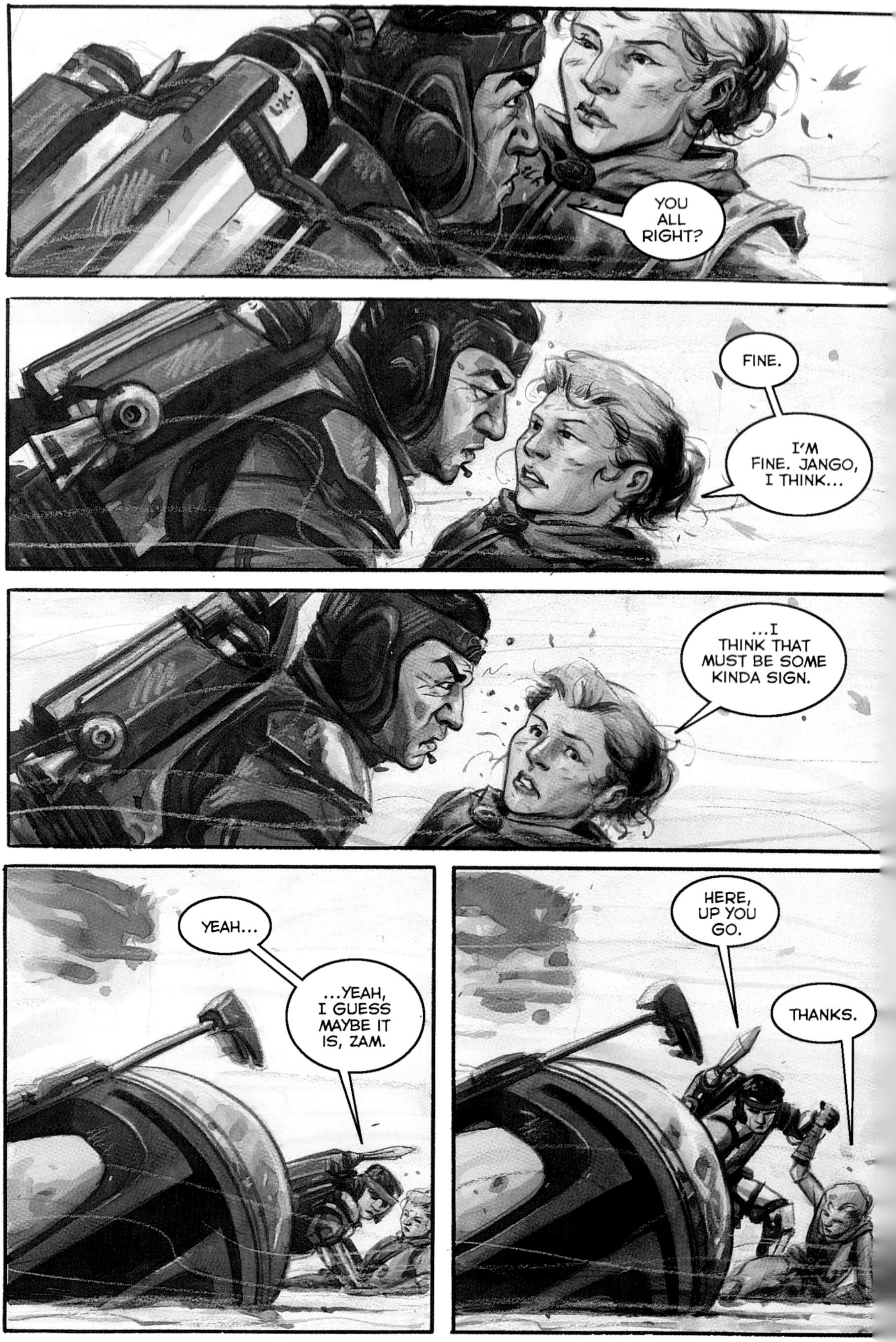
YOU ALL RIGHT?
FINE.
I'M FINE. JANGO, I THINK...
...I THINK THAT MUST BE SOME KINDA SIGN.
YEAH...
...YEAH, I GUESS MAYBE IT IS, ZAM.
HERE, UP YOU GO.
THANKS.

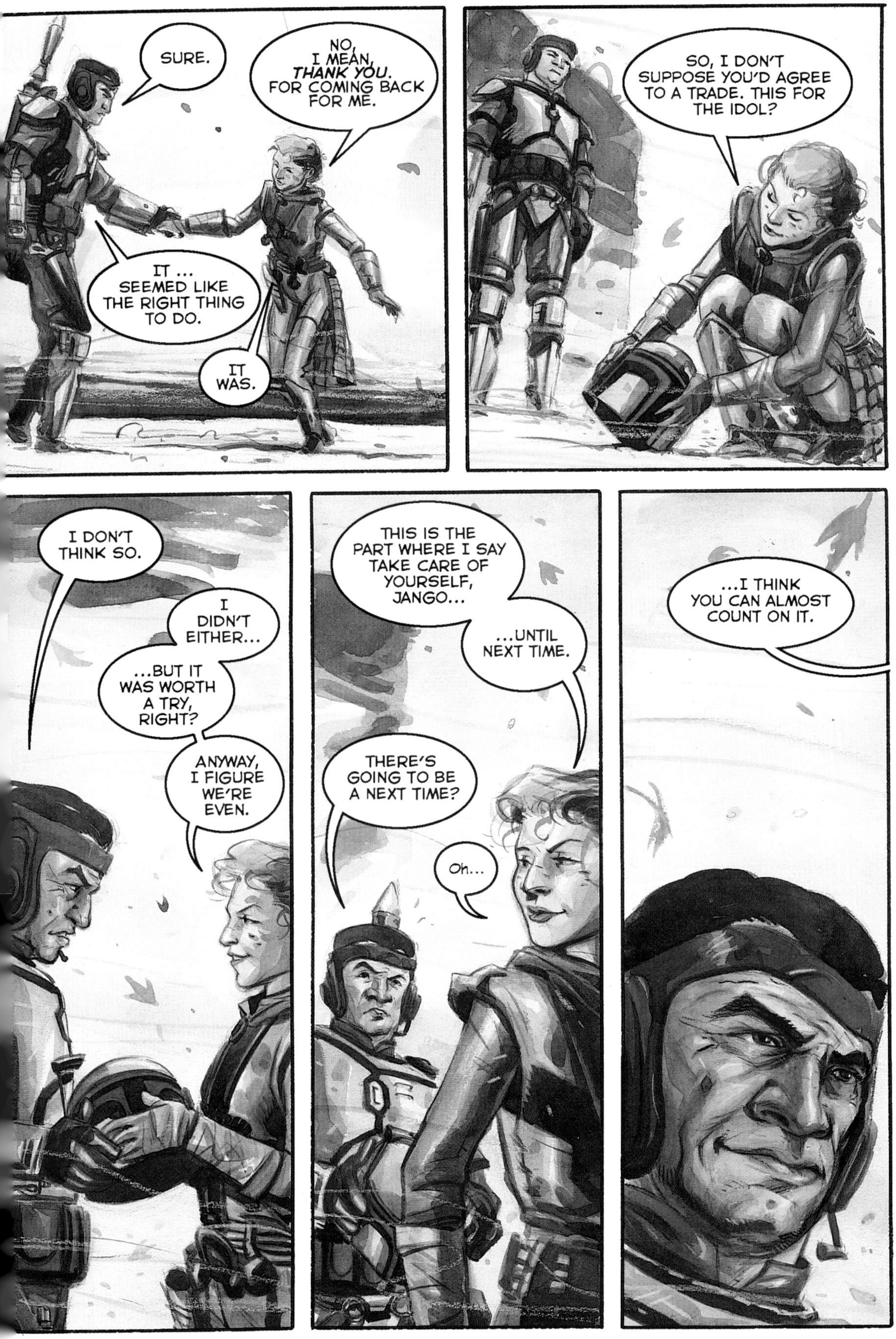
SURE.
NO, I MEAN, *THANK YOU.* FOR COMING BACK FOR ME.
IT ... SEEMED LIKE THE RIGHT THING TO DO.
IT WAS.
SO, I DON'T SUPPOSE YOU'D AGREE TO A TRADE. THIS FOR THE IDOL?
I DON'T THINK SO.
I DIDN'T EITHER...
...BUT IT WAS WORTH A TRY, RIGHT?
ANYWAY, I FIGURE WE'RE EVEN.
THIS IS THE PART WHERE I SAY TAKE CARE OF YOURSELF, JANGO...
...UNTIL NEXT TIME.
THERE'S GOING TO BE A NEXT TIME?
Oh...
...I THINK YOU CAN ALMOST COUNT ON IT.

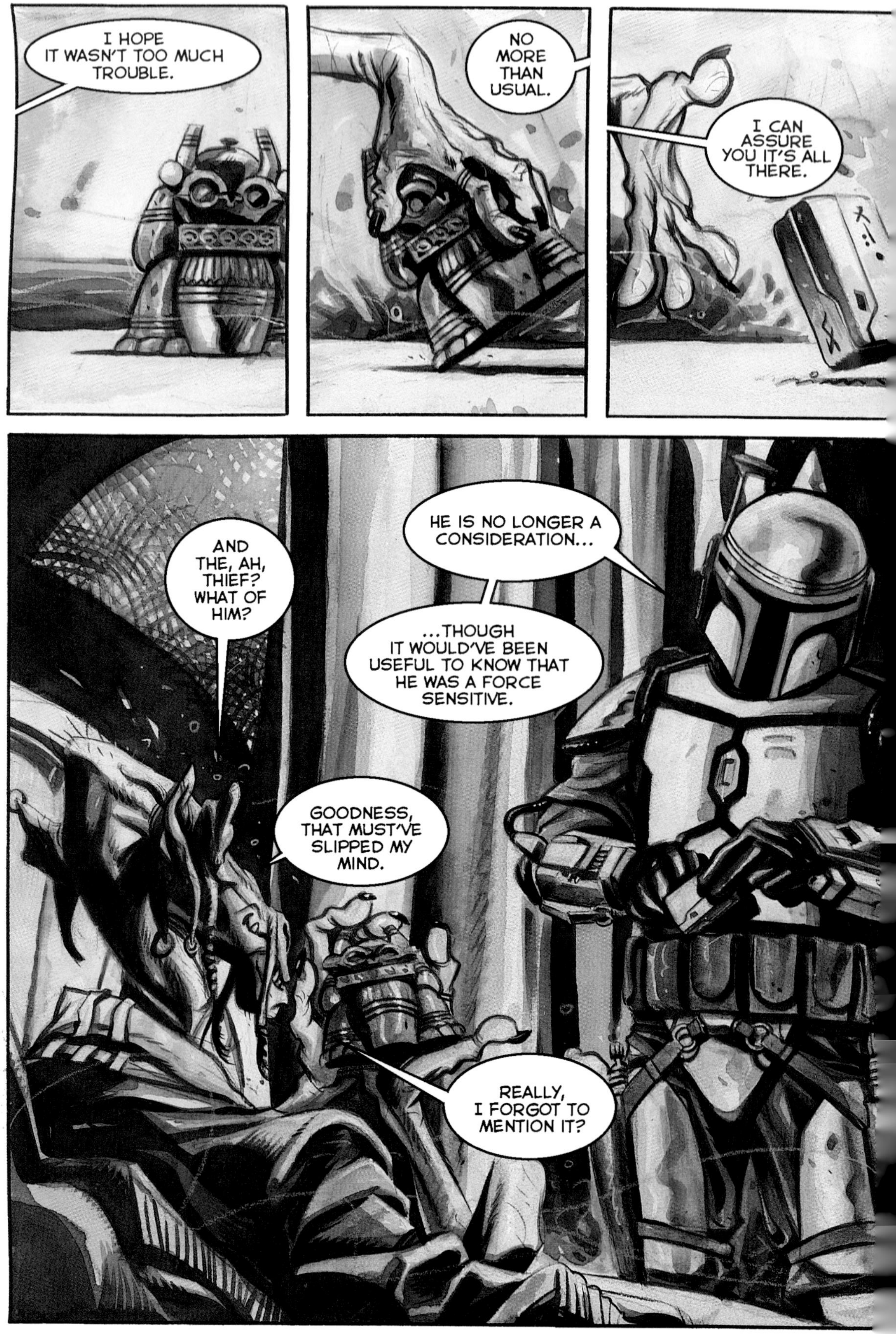
I HOPE IT WASN'T TOO MUCH TROUBLE.
NO MORE THAN USUAL.
I CAN ASSURE YOU IT'S ALL THERE.
AND THE, AH, THIEF? WHAT OF HIM?
HE IS NO LONGER A CONSIDERATION...
...THOUGH IT WOULD'VE BEEN USEFUL TO KNOW THAT HE WAS A FORCE SENSITIVE.
GOODNESS, THAT MUST'VE SLIPPED MY MIND.
REALLY, I FORGOT TO MENTION IT?

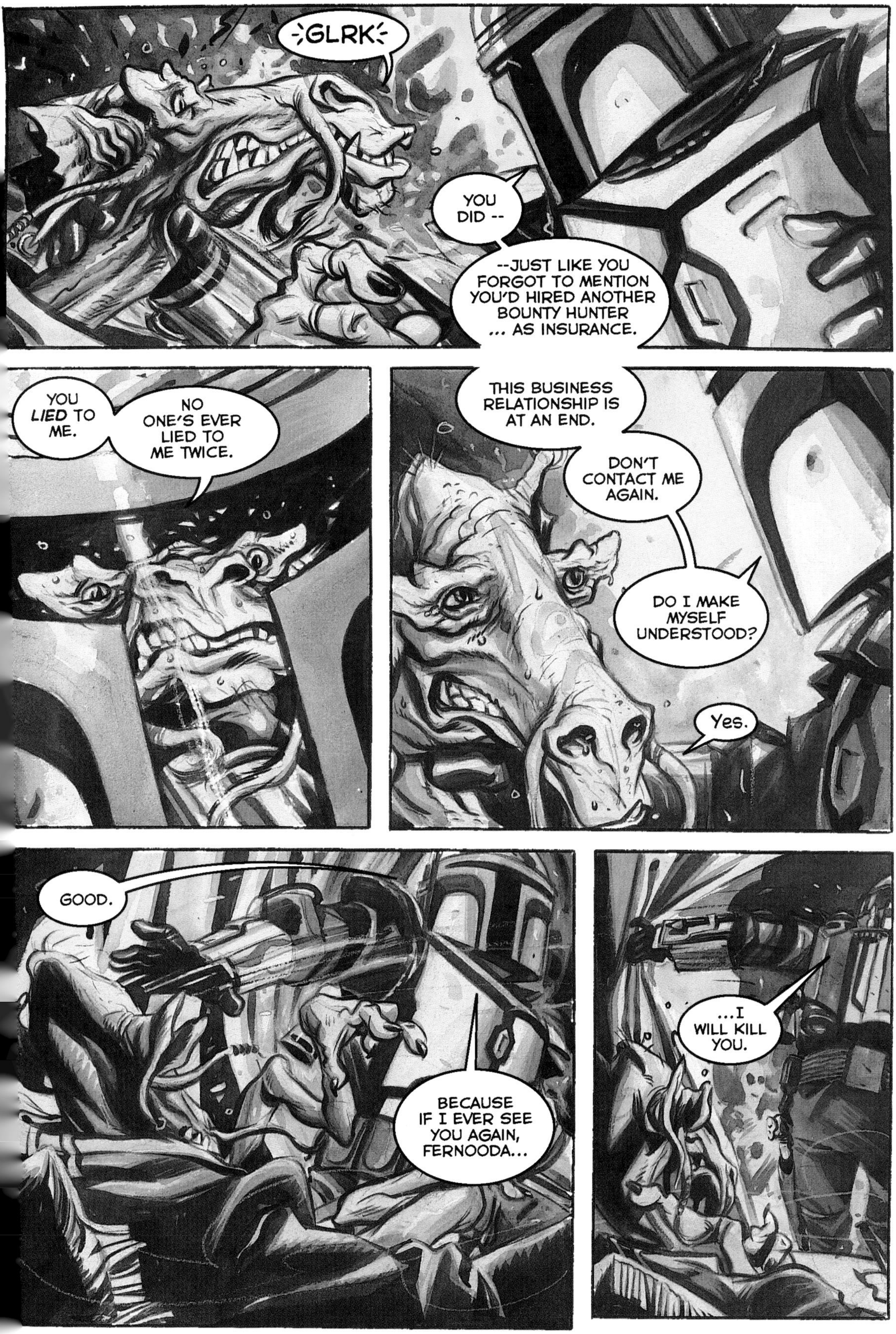
GLRK
YOU DID --
--JUST LIKE YOU FORGOT TO MENTION YOU'D HIRED ANOTHER BOUNTY HUNTER ... AS INSURANCE.
YOU *LIED* TO ME.
NO ONE'S EVER LIED TO ME TWICE.
THIS BUSINESS RELATIONSHIP IS AT AN END.
DON'T CONTACT ME AGAIN.
DO I MAKE MYSELF UNDERSTOOD?
Yes.
GOOD.
BECAUSE IF I EVER SEE YOU AGAIN, FERNOODA...
...I WILL KILL YOU.

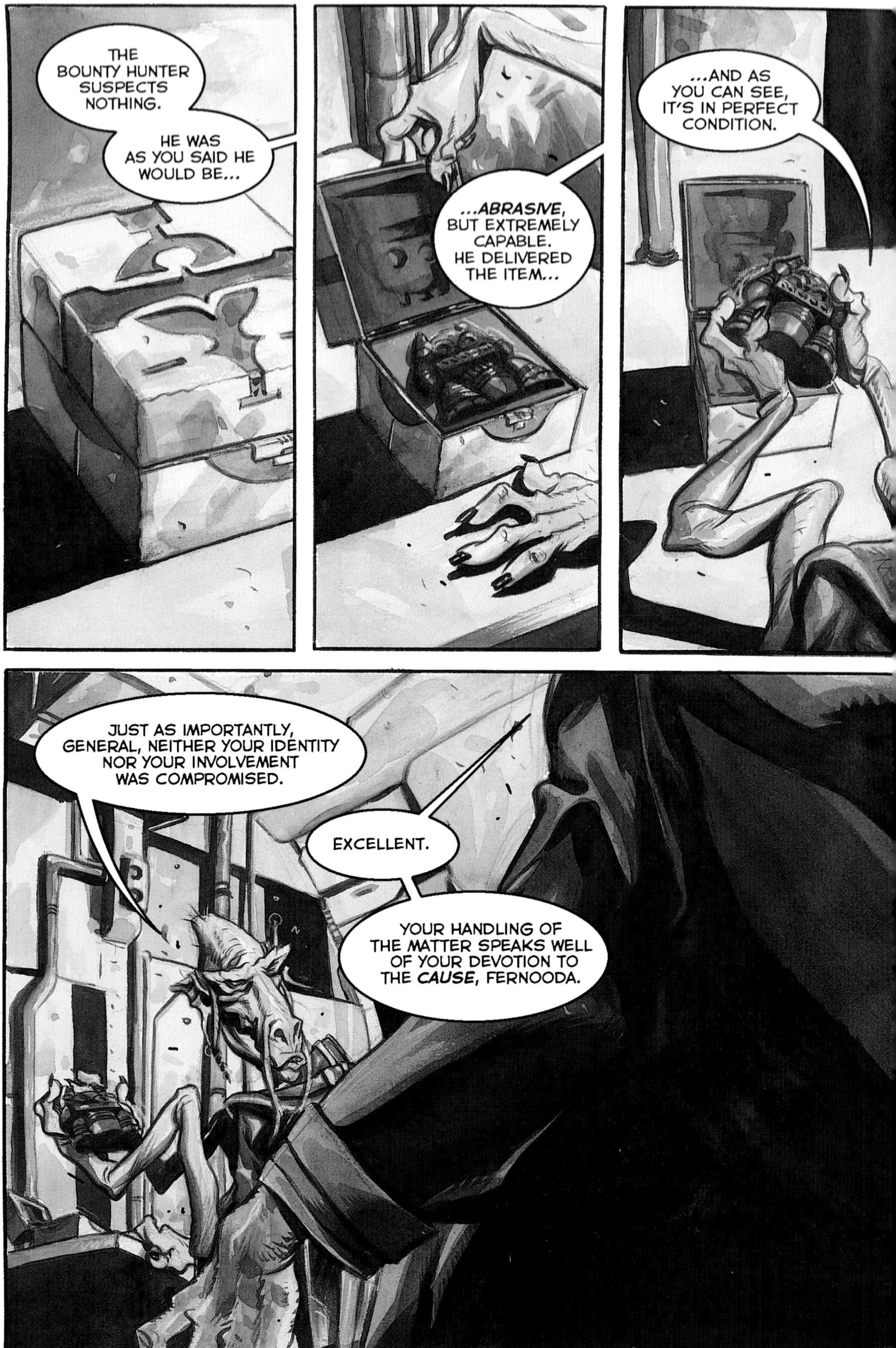
THE BOUNTY HUNTER SUSPECTS NOTHING.
HE WAS AS YOU SAID HE WOULD BE...
...*ABRASIVE*, BUT EXTREMELY CAPABLE. HE DELIVERED THE ITEM...
...AND AS YOU CAN SEE, IT'S IN PERFECT CONDITION.
JUST AS IMPORTANTLY, GENERAL, NEITHER YOUR IDENTITY NOR YOUR INVOLVEMENT WAS COMPROMISED.
EXCELLENT.
YOUR HANDLING OF THE MATTER SPEAKS WELL OF YOUR DEVOTION TO THE *CAUSE*, FERNOODA.

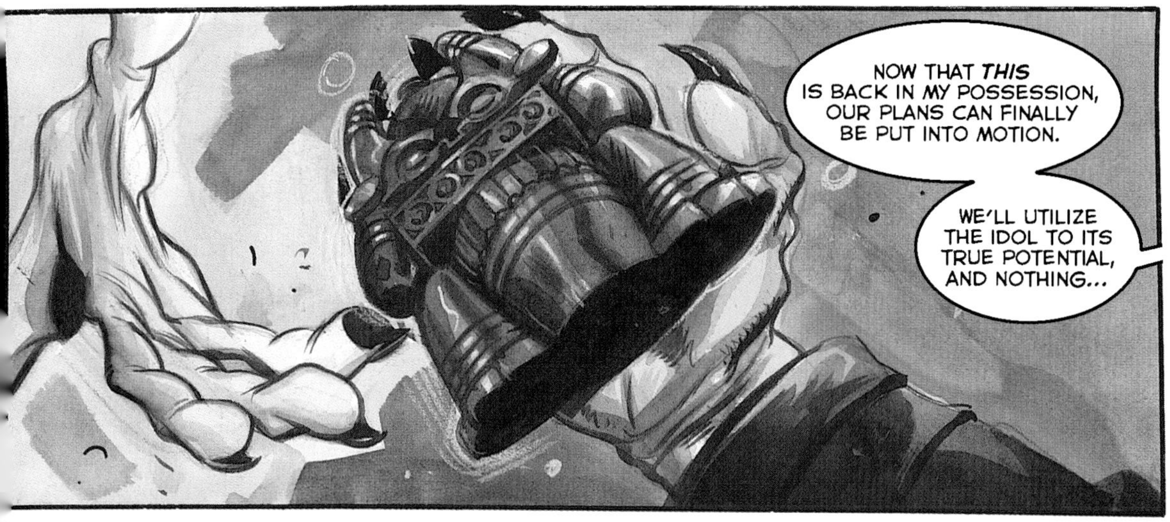
NOW THAT *THIS* IS BACK IN MY POSSESSION, OUR PLANS CAN FINALLY BE PUT INTO MOTION.
WE'LL UTILIZE THE IDOL TO ITS TRUE POTENTIAL, AND NOTHING...

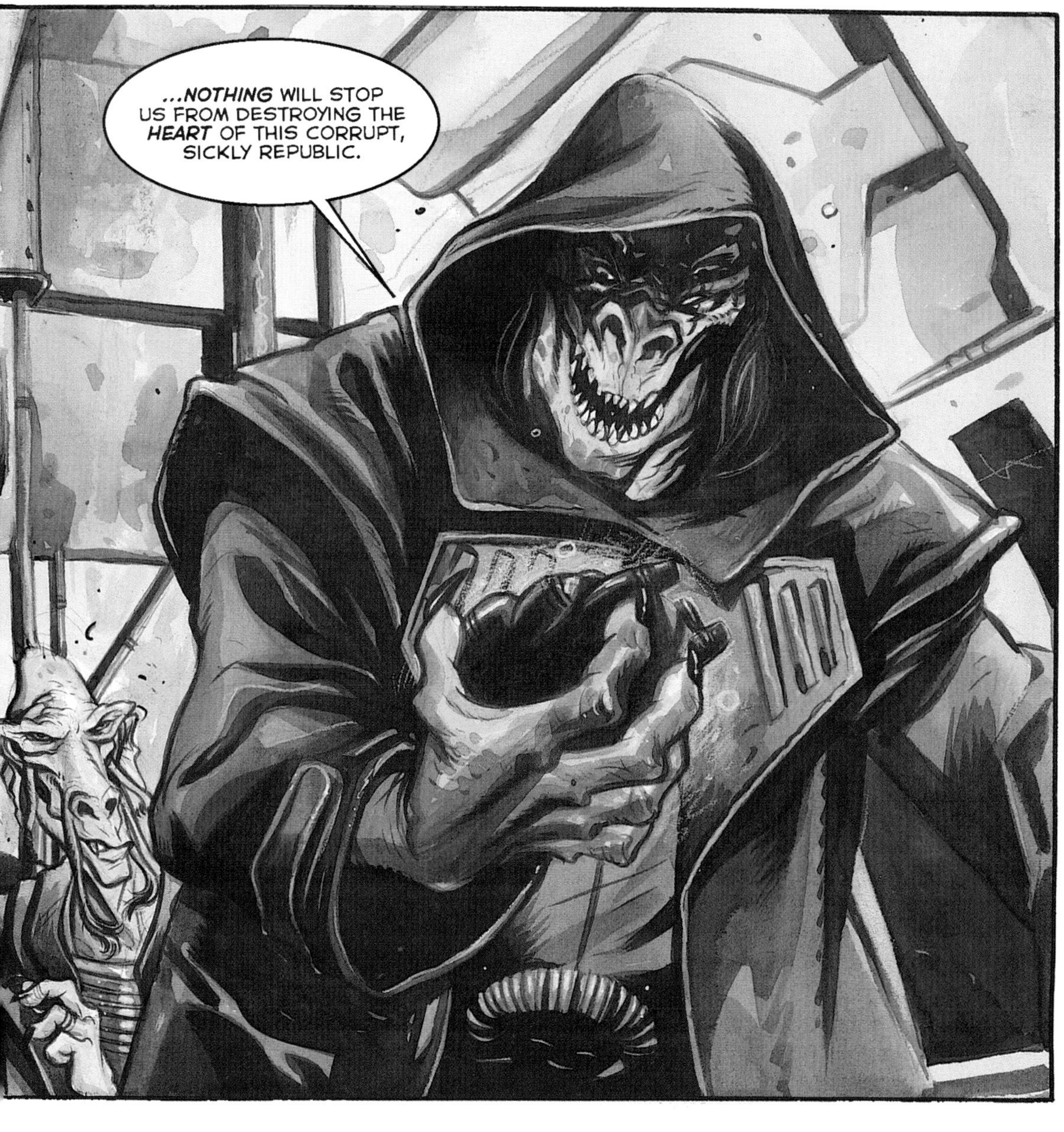
...*NOTHING* WILL STOP US FROM DESTROYING THE *HEART* OF THIS CORRUPT, SICKLY REPUBLIC.

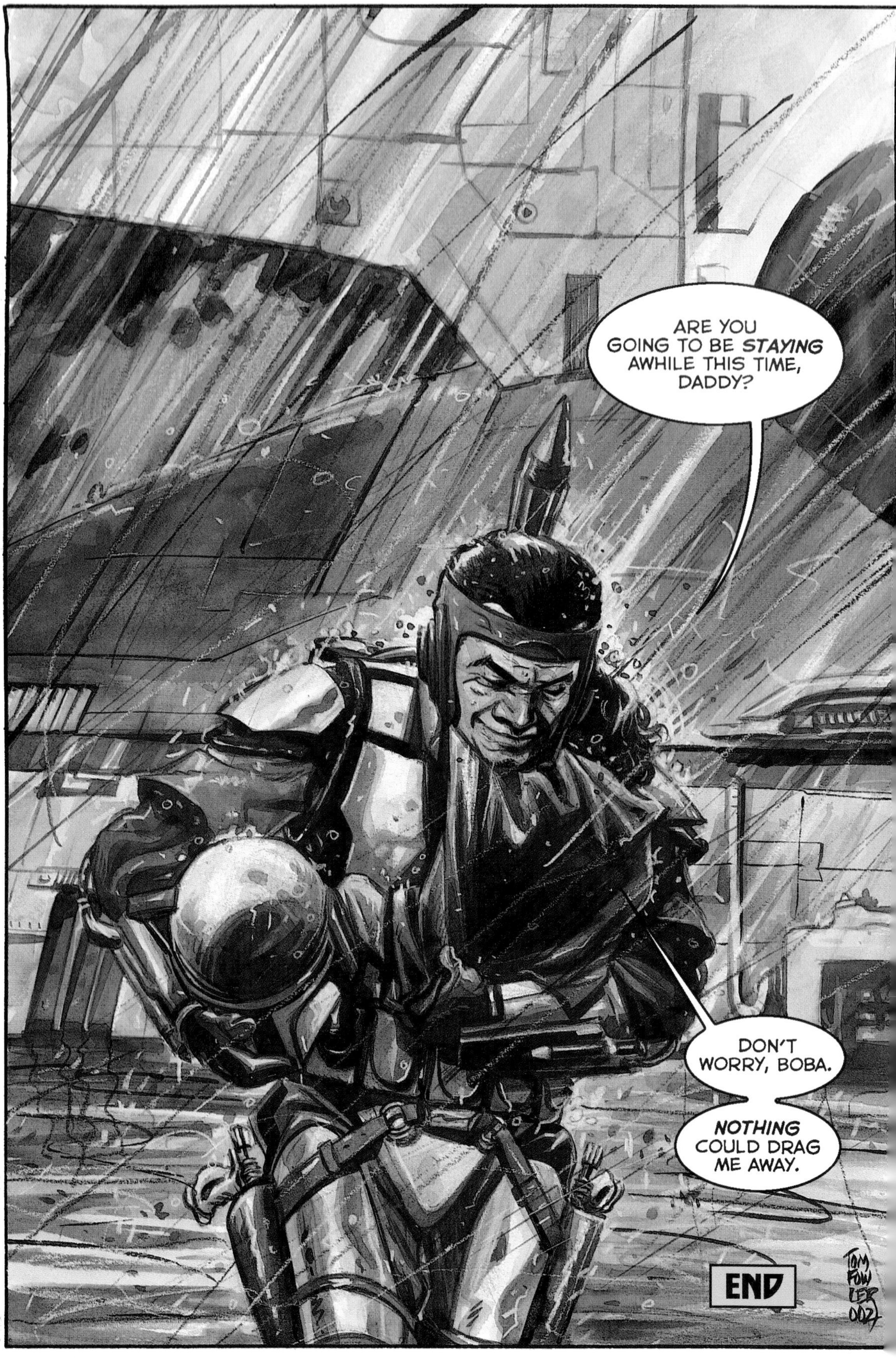
ARE YOU GOING TO BE *STAYING* AWHILE THIS TIME, DADDY?
DON'T WORRY, BOBA.
NOTHING COULD DRAG ME AWAY.
END
TOM FOWLER 002

STAR WARS *TIMELINE*

GRAPHIC NOVELS AND TRADE PAPERBACKS FROM DARK HORSE COMICS

For more information go to www.darkhorse.com

TALES OF THE SITH ERA 25,000-1000 YEARS BEFORE STAR WARS: A NEW HOPE

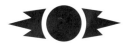

TALES OF THE JEDI
THE GOLDEN AGE OF THE SITH
Anderson • Carrasco, Jr. • Gossett
ISBN: 1-56971-229-8 $16.95
FALL OF THE SITH EMPIRE
Anderson • Heike • Carrasco, Jr.
ISBN: 1-56971-320-0 $14 .95
KNIGHTS OF THE OLD REPUBLIC
Veitch • Gossett
ISBN: 1-56971-020-1 $14.95
THE FREEDON NADD UPRISING
Veitch • Akins • Rodier
ISBN: 1-56971-307-3 $5.95
DARK LORDS OF THE SITH
Veitch • Anderson • Gossett
ISBN: 1-56971-095-3 $17.95
THE SITH WAR
Anderson • Carrasco, Jr.
ISBN: 1-56971-173-9 $17.95

STAR WARS
TALES OF THE JEDI
REDEMPTION

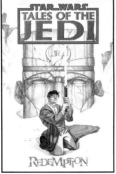

****REDEMPTION***
Anderson • Gossett • Pepoy • McDaniel
ISBN: 1-56971-535-1 $14.95

STAR WARS
JEDI vs SITH

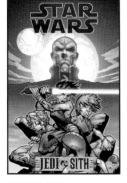

****JEDI VS. SITH***
Macan • Bachs • Fernandez
ISBN: 1-56971-649-8 $15.95

PREQUEL ERA 1000-0 YEARS BEFORE STAR WARS: A NEW HOPE

***JEDI COUNCIL**
ACTS OF WAR
Stradley • Fabbri • Vecchia
ISBN: 1-56971-539-4 $12.95

STAR WARS
JEDI COUNCIL
ACTS OF WAR

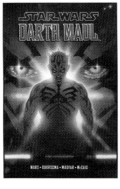

***DARTH MAUL**
Marz • Duursema • Magyar • Struzan
ISBN: 1-56971-542-4 $12.95

STAR WARS
DARTH MAUL
MARZ • DUURSEMA • MAGYAR • McCAIG

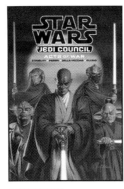

PRELUDE TO REBELLION
Strnad • Winn • Jones
ISBN: 1-56971-448-7 $14.95
OUTLANDER
Truman • Leonardi • Rio
ISBN: 1-56971-514-9 $14.95
***JEDI COUNCIL**
EMMISSARIES TO MALASTARE
Truman • Duursema • Others
ISBN: 1-56971-545-9 $15.95

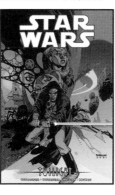

STAR WARS
TWILIGHT

STAR WARS: TWILIGHT
Ostrander • Duursema • Magyar
ISBN: 1-56971-558-0 $12.95
EPISODE 1 —
THE PHANTOM MENACE
Gilroy • Damaggio • Williamson
ISBN: 1-56971-359-6 $12.95
EPISODE 1 —
THE PHANTOM MENACE ADVENTURES
ISBN: 1-56971-443-6 $12.95

MANGA EDITIONS
Translated into English
EPISODE 1 —
THE PHANTOM MENACE
George Lucas • Kia Asamiya
VOLUME 1
ISBN: 1-56971-483-5 $9.95
VOLUME 2
ISBN: 1-56971-484-3 $9.95

STAR WARS
JANGO FETT

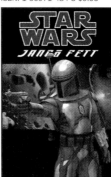

***JANGO FETT**
Marz • Fowler
ISBN: 1-56971-623-4 $5.95

STAR WARS
ZAM WESELL

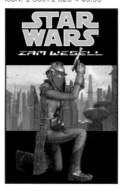

***ZAM WESELL**
Marz • Naifeh
ISBN: 1-56971-624-2 $5.95

STAR WARS
EPISODE II
ATTACK OF THE CLONES

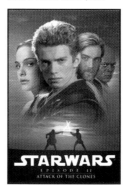

EPISODE 2 —
ATTACK OF THE CLONES
Gilroy • Duursema • Kryssing • McCaig
ISBN: 1-56971-609-9 $17.95
DROIDS
THE KALARBA ADVENTURES
Thorsland • Windham • Gibson
ISBN: 1-56971-064-3 $17.95
REBELLION
Windham • Gibson
ISBN: 1-56971-224-7 $14.95

JABBA THE HUTT
THE ART OF THE DEAL
Woodring • Wetherell • Sheldon
ISBN: 1-56971-310-3 $9.95
***UNDERWORLD**
THE YAVIN VASSILIKA
Kennedy • Meglia
ISBN: 1-56971-618-8 $14.95
CLASSIC STAR WARS
HAN SOLO AT STARS' END
Goodwin • Alcala
ISBN: 1-56971-254-9 $6.95
BOBA FETT
ENEMY OF THE EMPIRE
Wagner • Gibson • Nadeau • Ezquerra
ISBN: 1-56971-407-X $12.95

TRILOGY ERA 0-5 YEARS AFTER STAR WARS: A NEW HOPE

***A NEW HOPE* SPECIAL EDITION**
Jones • Barreto • Williamson
ISBN: 1-56971-213-1 $9.95
MANGA EDITIONS
Translated into English
A NEW HOPE
George Lucas • Hisao Tamaki
VOLUME 1
ISBN: 1-56971-362-6 $9.95
VOLUME 2
ISBN: 1-56971-363-4 $9.95
VOLUME 3
ISBN: 1-56971-364-2 $9.95
VOLUME 4
ISBN: 1-56971-365-0 $9.95
VADER'S QUEST
Macan • Gibbons
ISBN: 1-56971-415-0 $11.95

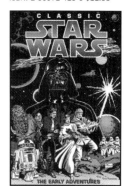

CLASSIC
STAR WARS
THE EARLY ADVENTURES

CLASSIC STAR WARS
THE EARLY ADVENTURES
Manning • Hoberg
ISBN: 1-56971-178-X $19.95
SPLINTER OF THE MIND'S EYE
Austin • Sprouse
ISBN: 1-56971-223-9 $14.95
CLASSIC STAR WARS
IN DEADLY PURSUIT
Goodwin • Williamson
ISBN: 1-56971-109-7 $16.95
THE EMPIRE STRIKES BACK SPECIAL EDITION
Goodwin • Williamson
ISBN: 1-56971-234-4 $9.95
MANGA EDITIONS
Translated into English
THE EMPIRE STRIKES BACK
George Lucas • Toshiki Kudo
VOLUME 1
ISBN: 1-56971-390-1 $9.95

AVAILABLE AT YOUR LOCAL COMICS SHOP OR BOOKSTORE
To find a comics shop in your area, call 1-888-266-4226
For more information or to order direct:
•On the web: www.darkhorse.com •E-mail: mailorder@darkhorse.com
•Phone: 1-800-862-0052 or (503) 652-9701 Mon.-Sat. 9 A.M. to 5 P.M. Pacific Time

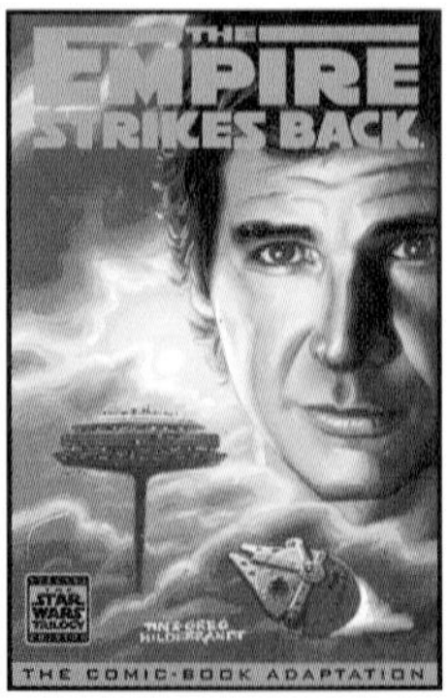
THE EMPIRE STRIKES BACK
THE COMIC-BOOK ADAPTATION

VOLUME 2
ISBN: 1-56971-391-X $9.95
VOLUME 3
ISBN: 1-56971-392-8 $9.95
VOLUME 4
ISBN: 1-56971-393-6 $9.95
CLASSIC STAR WARS
THE REBEL STORM
Goodwin • Williamson
ISBN: 1-56971-106-2 $16.95
CLASSIC STAR WARS
ESCAPE TO HOTH
Goodwin • Williamson
ISBN: 1-56971-093-7 $16.95
SHADOWS OF THE EMPIRE
SHADOWS OF THE EMPIRE
Wagner • Plunkett • Russell
ISBN: 1-56971-183-6 $17.95
RETURN OF THE JEDI
SPECIAL EDITION
Goodwin • Williamson
ISBN: 1-56971-235-2 $9.95
MANGA EDITIONS
Translated into English
RETURN OF THE JEDI
George Lucas • Shin-ichi Hiromoto

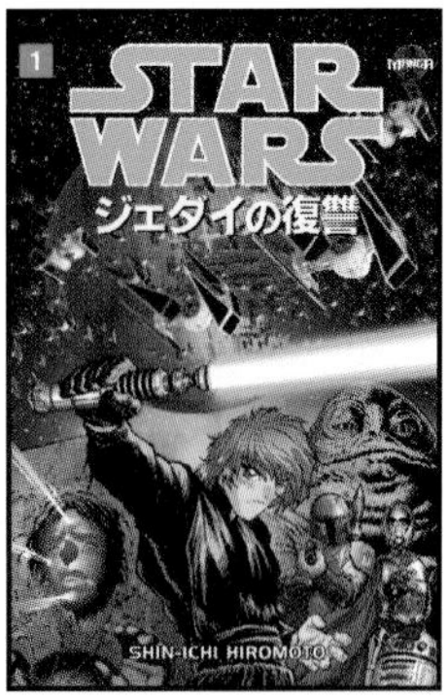
STAR WARS
ジェダイの復讐
SHIN-ICHI HIROMOTO

VOLUME 1
ISBN: 1-56971-394-4 $9.95
VOLUME 2
ISBN: 1-56971-395-2 $9.95
VOLUME 3
ISBN: 1-56971-396-0 $9.95
VOLUME 4
ISBN: 1-56971-397-9 $9.95

CLASSIC SPIN-OFF ERA 5-25 YEARS AFTER STAR WARS: A NEW HOPE

MARA JADE
BY THE EMPEROR'S HAND
Zahn • Stackpole • Ezquerra
ISBN: 1-56971-401-0 $15.95

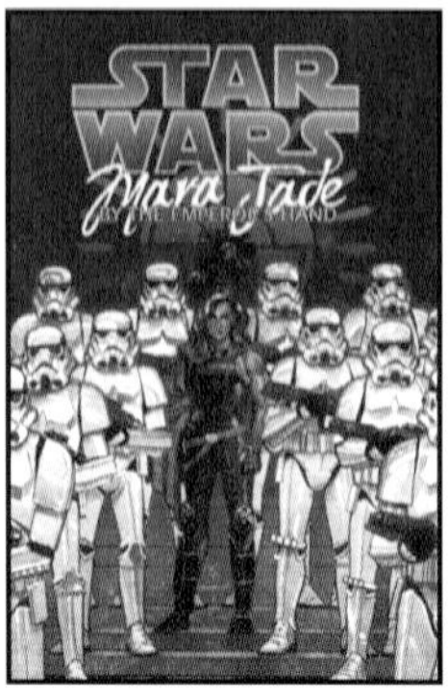
STAR WARS
Mara Jade

SHADOWS OF THE EMPIRE
EVOLUTION
Perry • Randall • Simmons
ISBN: 1-56971-441-X $14.95
X-WING ROGUE SQUADRON
THE PHANTOM AFFAIR
Stackpole • Macan • Biukovic
ISBN: 1-56971-251-4 $12.95

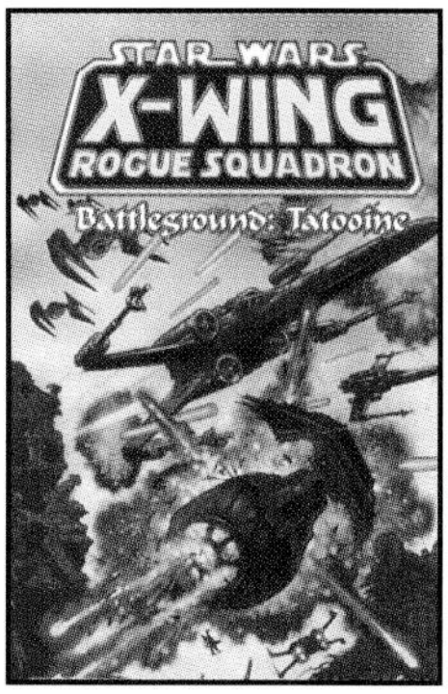
STAR WARS
X-WING
ROGUE SQUADRON
Battleground: Tatooine

BATTLEGROUND: TATOOINE
Stackpole • Strnad • Nadeau • Ensign
ISBN: 1-56971-276-X $12.95
THE WARRIOR PRINCESS
Stackpole • Tolson • Nadeau • Ensign
ISBN: 1-56971-330-8 $12.95

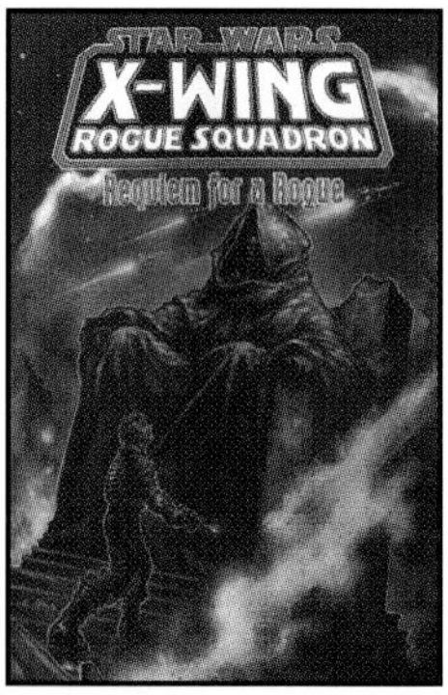
STAR WARS
X-WING
ROGUE SQUADRON
Requiem for a Rogue

REQUIEM FOR A ROGUE
Stackpole • Strnad • Barr • Erskine
ISBN: 1-56971-331-6 $12.95
IN THE EMPIRE'S SERVICE
Stackpole • Nadeau • Ensign
ISBN: 1-56971-383-9 $12.95
BLOOD AND HONOR
Stackpole • Crespo • Hall • Martin
ISBN: 1-56971-387-1 $12.95
MASQUERADE
Stackpole • Johnson • Martin
ISBN: 1-56971-487-8 $12.95

MANDATORY RETIREMENT
Stackpole • Crespo • Nadeau
ISBN: 1-56971-492-4 $12.95
THE THRAWN TRILOGY
HEIR TO THE EMPIRE
Baron • Vatine • Blanchard
ISBN: 1-56971-202-6 $19.95
DARK FORCE RISING
Baron • Dodson • Nowlan
ISBN: 1-56971-269-7 $17.95
THE LAST COMMAND
Baron • Biukovic • Shanower
ISBN: 1-56971-378-2 $17.95
DARK EMPIRE
DARK EMPIRE
Veitch • Kennedy
ISBN: 1-56971-073-2 $17.95
DARK EMPIRE II
Veitch • Kennedy
ISBN: 1-56971-119-4 $17.95
EMPIRE'S END
Veitch • Baikie
ISBN: 1-56971-306-5 $5.95

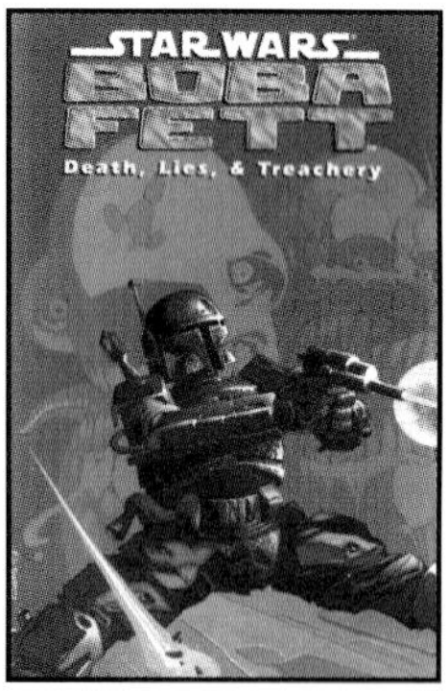
STAR WARS
BOBA FETT
Death, Lies, & Treachery

BOBA FETT
DEATH, LIES,
& TREACHERY
Wagner • Kennedy
ISBN: 1-56971-311-1 $12.95
CRIMSON EMPIRE
CRIMSON EMPIRE
Richardson • Stradley • Gulacy • Russell
ISBN: 1-56971-355-3 $17.95

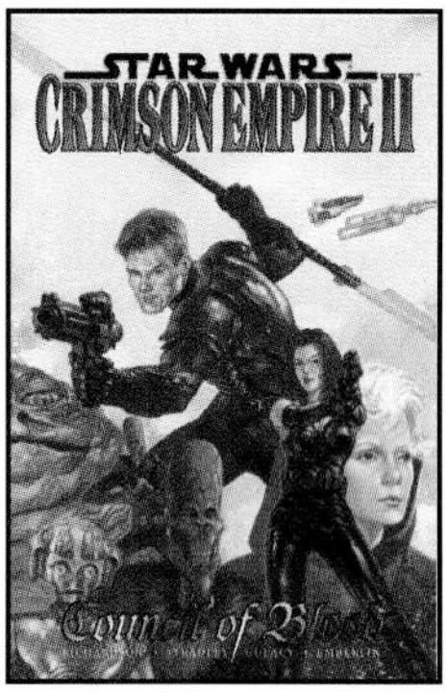
STAR WARS
CRIMSON EMPIRE II
Council of Blood

COUNCIL OF BLOOD
Richardson • Stradley • Gulacy • Emberlin
ISBN: 1-56971-410-X $17.95
JEDI ACADEMY
LEVIATHAN
Anderson • Carrasco • Heike
ISBN: 1-56971-456-8 $11.95

THE NEW JEDI ORDER ERA 25+ YEARS AFTER STAR WARS: A NEW HOPE

UNION
Stackpole • Teranishi • Chuckry
ISBN: 1-56971-464-9 $12.95

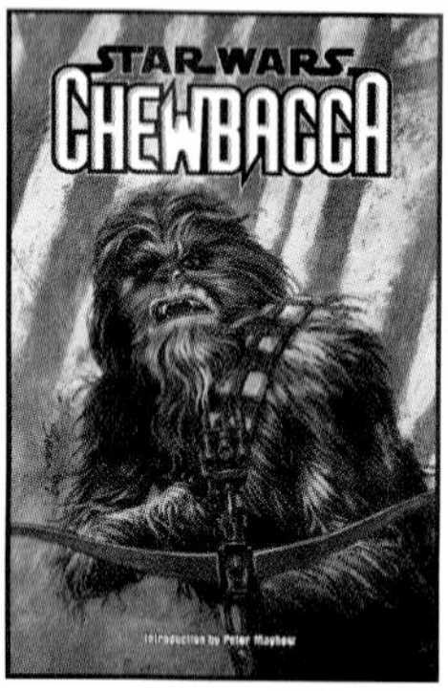
STAR WARS
CHEWBACCA

CHEWBACCA
Macan • Duursema • Others
ISBN: 1-56971-515-7 $12.95

INFINITIES — DOES NOT APPLY TO TIMELINE

***TALES VOLUME 1**
Marz • Plunkett • Duursema • Others
ISBN: 1-56971-619-6 $19.95
***INFINITIES — A NEW HOPE**
Warner • Johnson • Snyder • Rio • Nelson
ISBN: 1-56971-648-X $12.95

BATTLE OF THE BOUNTY HUNTERS
POP-UP COMIC BOOK
Windham • Moeller
ISBN: 1-56971-129-1 $17.95
DARK FORCES
Prose novellas, heavily illustrated
SOLDIER FOR THE EMPIRE
Dietz • Williams
hardcover edition
ISBN: 1-56971-155-0 $24.95
paperback edition
ISBN: 1-56971-348-0 $14.95
REBEL AGENT
Dietz • Tucker
hardcover edition
ISBN: 1-56971-156-9 $24.95
paperback edition
ISBN: 1-56971-400-2 $14.95
JEDI KNIGHT
Dietz • Dorman
hardcover edition
ISBN: 1-56971-157-7 $24.95
paperback edition
ISBN: 1-56971-433-9 $14.95

SPANS MULTIPLE ERAS

BOUNTY HUNTERS
Truman • Schultz • Stradley • Mangels
ISBN: 1-56971-467-3 $12.95

* *New*

•Prices and availability subject to change without notice

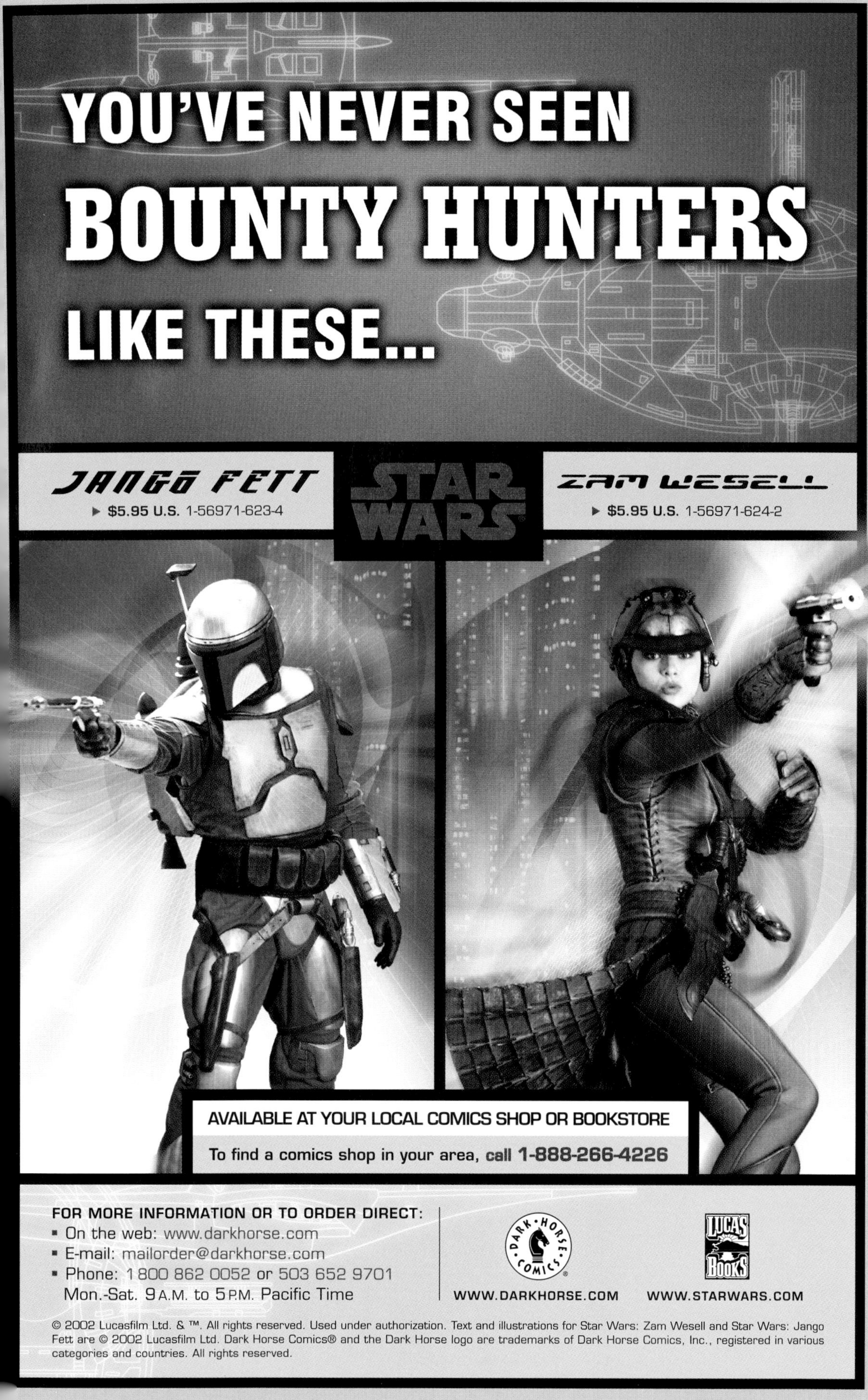
YOU'VE NEVER SEEN
BOUNTY HUNTERS
LIKE THESE...
JANGO FETT
▶ $5.95 U.S. 1-56971-623-4
STAR WARS
ZAM WESELL
▶ $5.95 U.S. 1-56971-624-2
AVAILABLE AT YOUR LOCAL COMICS SHOP OR BOOKSTORE
To find a comics shop in your area, call 1-888-266-4226
FOR MORE INFORMATION OR TO ORDER DIRECT:
▪ On the web: www.darkhorse.com
▪ E-mail: mailorder@darkhorse.com
▪ Phone: 1 800 862 0052 or 503 652 9701
Mon.-Sat. 9 A.M. to 5 P.M. Pacific Time
DARK HORSE COMICS
WWW.DARKHORSE.COM
LUCAS BOOKS
WWW.STARWARS.COM
© 2002 Lucasfilm Ltd. & ™. All rights reserved. Used under authorization. Text and illustrations for Star Wars: Zam Wesell and Star Wars: Jango Fett are © 2002 Lucasfilm Ltd. Dark Horse Comics® and the Dark Horse logo are trademarks of Dark Horse Comics, Inc., registered in various categories and countries. All rights reserved.

VE I SLAVE I SLAVE I SLAVE I SLAV

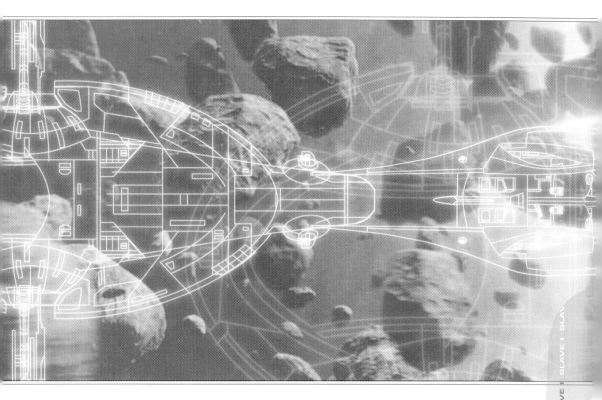